Jumbled Up

(An *In the Jingle Jangle Jungle*

Companion Piece)

Joel Gion

ISBN: 979-8-9987070-0-1

Cover and inside image: Jonathan Kochan
Cover design: Galine Tumasova

a Bandied Book

The First "Blow It"

I lie on my floor mattress in my second-story apartment, watching the sun come up from behind the jumbled rows of neighboring Victorian rooftops while listening to the current at-the-tone-time-correct comedown track, "6 O'clock" by The Verve. After I don't know how long, finally, my night's speed wire and E discombobulation combo slowly starts to loosen its grip, loosening down further, and then looser still, until mercifully, I gently doze off five minutes before my work alarm goes off.

There's something about committing to the act of sleep, even if it's for only thirty seconds, that somehow cleans your chemical slate, and you make a metamorphosis of cosmic traveler into a shackled prisoner of the hangover dungeon. Now, after my five-minute night sleep, I'd gone and lost my fluid night-into-day lucid state and was now rebirthed and mind blown into a spit wad of fragility.

So, despite my living on the corner of San Francisco's Waller and Masonic, a mere block away from where I work on Haight Street, by the time I pull the rest of whatever is left of myself together, I am yet again more than fifteen minutes late. I love my job at Reckless Records and don't want to lose it, but in recent days, I was at least that late every day.

I show up with that pasty, extra-pale, all-nighter-into-

1

the-following-day glow that's great for hair, but everything below my bangs is just like it sounds and is causing everyone else on the morning shift to get that now-familiar worried look. I'm well liked around Reckless, and despite often making it harder on everyone else by my altered states, these were indeed the days of raves and line-snorting musicians, and both were understood as signs o' the times. This was the fabled Haight Street during its 1994 season, after all, and on some level, I was "going for it" so British management and the rest of the indie music enthusiast hodgepodge staff didn't have to. They were all together now, rooting for me to not blow the gig permanently, but today I came to work accessorized with my own knockout bell and set of ropes on my back.

By an act of the alien gods, the store manager has taken the day off, and so, upon covert private evaluation, my coworkers decide the best place for me is to be sequestered away from the public eye by having me rotate the entire vinyl back stock to make more shelf space for the incoming vinyl new arrivals. Unfortunately, even this simplest of tasks isn't a good idea either, and with my crashed and still-burning mind, I mistakenly rotate all the shelf stock from top to bottom instead of side to side, resulting in completely rearranging the numerical filing system totally out of order. I'm then to spend the same amount of cold-sweat time putting it all back together, and it's just as I'm finishing the now hours-long task to the very comedown-unfriendly hypnotic sounds of The Orb's "Puffy Little Clouds" that Stephanie strides into the store, looking excited. That is until, just like my coworkers, she sees me up close. Stephanie looks like a colorized young Claire Bloom in a tight Breton striped top and James Dean blue jeans with an oxblood leather belt color coordinated with her *Rosemary's Baby* Vidal Sassoon hairstyle.

It only takes a mini-exchange to realize that I'm cooking in the breeze, but I'm still holding on to the last card left in my one-card deck, I'm kinda for pretty sure, which is the "first date" idea I came up with the day before. "Hey, are you busy tomorrow night?" She looks a little surprised I'm going ahead into date mode, seeing that I'm in the middle of completely blowing it and all. "*Easy Rider* is playing at The Red Vic. Wanna go?"

"Uh … sure, okay. I've never seen it. I know I'm supposed to have, right?"

"Yeah, it's pretty classic, one of my favorite movies," I say, standing perfectly diagonal. *Wait, what just happened? She said yes?*

The next night, I arrive at Upper Haight Street's Red Vic Movie House about ten minutes before showtime. She's nowhere in sight from either direction, so I'm wondering if she'd come to her senses since yesterday and I'm actually going to this alone. I stride across the street to the Liquid Experience liquor store and buy a pint of Jim Beam whisky. Even if she is still coming, what's wrong with a little first-date icebreaker, I tell myself.

As I cross back over the hippie Sesame Street, I slide the bottle into the inside chest pocket of my black leather cafe racer jacket. It's from this middle-of-the-street vantage point that I see Stephanie coming down the block. We exchange waves and smiles as we arrive synchronized at the back of the growing theater line. As you can

3

imagine, this type of film goes over pretty big on Haight Street. With not much time for small talk, we buy tickets and walk straight into the arthouse theater.

The lights are already slowly dimming as we enter, leaving us just enough time to see that the only empty area left is down in the front row. After quickly settling into the fresh darkness, I sneak a peek and see the flickering projector light reflect brightly in her eyes as old celluloid film stock blares bright daytime onto the screen. The scattered audience chatter dissipates, and we all unify in a group transition into cinematic reality.

I've already seen this film so many times now, mostly with my older brother, Paul. He was surely the "rough-and-tumble" one of the two of us. He was the mechanic, the mister fix-it, and the brawler. By now he'd graduated nicely into a modern-day "one-percenter"-style biker and had all the kustom bike chops to make for a real-deal yesterday's sixties biker today. His garage was packed full of enough vintage motorcycle parts to construct five outlaw bikes without even having to leave the structure. Some years later, even the Hell's Angels would recognize the motorcycle club he would found and name The Death Traps.

A few times a year, I'd find an excuse (which was when I would be finding myself literally going off the rails) to go up to "the sticks," where he now lived, so we could go through his crazy extensive sixties and seventies biker movie collection while making Wizard's Staffs out of Coors beer thirty-packs. (A Wizard's Staff is the act of taking every successive beer can personally drunk in a single session and duct taping the tops and bottoms

4

together as you go. Once your row, or staff, of accumulated empty beer cans reaches any length above your head, this signifies that you have drunk enough beer to have attained the capabilities and the all-knowingness level of a wizard.) I'd play along like I understood the motorcycle specs he'd point out on the screen, but for me, these films were much more about the fashion show of sixties leather jackets, tops with extra-wide stripes, and all various types of psychedelic rebel fashion accessories. Visiting my brother on these trips was like a righteous sabbatical, an escape from the city to recharge myself at the outlaw temple. It was weirdly Zen.

Easy Rider begins, and experiencing this film for the first time not in the presence of the already converted, I weirdly find myself starting to feel a slight sense of uncertainty. This time it's playing out slower than I remember, and somehow, Peter Fonda's ultra-cool character now seems slightly awkward in a way I hadn't recognized in all my previous viewings. Even Hopper is somehow extra buffoonish. Part of me wishes an event were coming up to rope her into the story, but it's not that kind of film. It's the kind of film you walk into already *in*. Like the line in the film, it does its own thing in its own time. Despite this, the following hippie commune portion is a very slow burn now, even for me. Hippies dropping out of society and starting communes in the middle of nowhere is by now a concept long gone from being a commentary on a new and alternative lifestyle, like it was back in 1969.

Mercifully, we finally make it to the introduction of Jack Nicholson's character, which also in a certain way kickstarts the whole thing into gear. From here on out, we are on a roll of all the scenes that make this the timeless classic it's famous for. I celebrate this new freedom along with Jack's on-screen character as he pulls out a pint of Jim Beam as I do the same thing and join him in his "Here's to the first of the day, fellas" toast. I then hand the bottle over to Stephanie. Without even looking away from the screen, she slowly shakes her head no.

I shrug and take another pull. The warm fuzzies begin to mingle-tingle in my tummy. As the three characters ride on motorcycles through an Arizona stretch of Route 66 along to The Holy Modal Rounders' swaying, orbit-less jug-time rag "I Wanna Be a Bird," I decide to let all the music interludes DJ my bottle tilts, and by the time Fonda delivers the famous ambiguous line, "We blew it," I'm about to join them.

The end of the film is here as Hopper flips the bird to some antagonistic, pickup-driving rednecks. Rightly the audience giggles—but after, when he's gunned down in return, the giggles strangely continue. *What's up with that?* I turn around wondering. Then, Fonda, seeing what has happened, immediately races back to the fallen Hopper. Seeing that he is dying fast, he scrambles back onto his motorcycle and races off for help, unfortunately going back in the direction of the rednecks. Somehow, despite the tragedy of the scene, the new humor vibe in the theater is gaining further momentum as someone shouts in an animated stoner tone, "You don't want to go back there, *maan*!" followed by more laughter. My own engine, now on a full tank of Kentucky bourbon, begins to run hot.

The chilling ending of the film finishes with Fonda

also being shot by the rednecks mid-ride, sending him flying through the air. This very moment is the ignition switch of the 1970s American New Wave cinema movement and its long-celebrated trend of fatalistic reality film endings. Suddenly, another voice shouts sarcastically in a Shaggy from Scooby-Doo accent, "Bhummer trip, maan!" Big group laughter. My own engine now explodes, along with the on-film bike bursting into flames lying along the side of the road.

Fully drunk, I stand up from my front-row-center seat and turn around to address the crowd. "You are all a bunch of cows! A bunch of cows! Mooo! Moooo! Mooooo!"

The final helicopter camera shot of the accident scene is rising far into the air on the screen behind me as the credits begin to roll and everything goes dark, leaving the end theme music, "Ballad of Easy Rider," to continue on in blackness as I march out of the theater solo.

As I sit waiting right outside on the curb, Stephanie is the first out the door. "*What* is wrong with you!"

I shake my head and look up, but before I can even answer, she's already turned around and walking away into the chilly Haight Street night.

Oh well, this is all only a movie.

An "A" Note

"Okay, if the rest of you wanna be on the record cover, then don't take a bad picture!" Anton and I have just met Matt Hollywood, Dean Taylor, and Brian Glaze in front of the Horseshoe Cafe in Lower Haight. Hellos are forgone as Anton holds a borrowed Polaroid camera in one hand while immediately firing off instructions with the other. Apparently, there are only five shots left in the instant camera, and we are making the *Methodrone* album cover with them here and now before Anton leaves tomorrow for LA to visit Bomp! Records owner and garage-rock impresario Greg Shaw. Being the first full-length album to be recorded by The Brian Jonestown Massacre, which had by now in '95 been in the can for over a year, turning in the record cover artwork is high on Anton's TCB list.

The sun is setting fast in purples and golds from behind a row of old Victorian apartment buildings as Anton instructs Brian to stand up against a wall outside the cafe. He aims, clicks, and shoots with a blasting flash, accompanied by the robotic sound of spitting photo paper. "Good."

He then revolves around to face Dean, starting with his upper torso, then followed by the rest of him. He seems to be in a constant state of intent. He stands with intent, he walks with intent; it's a permanent residence of at-the-ready. Ready and in-it-to-win-it and usually before

8

the rest of us knows it's even an *it* to be won. "Okay, Dean—record cover, let's go," he says, more like he's commentating on the action rather than commanding it. He clicks, and the camera sticks out a paper tongue at Dean. He peels it off and shakes it.

"All riiight," he says approvingly as Dean's "face" face bleeds into focus.

"Where's Matt?"

Matt is slowly disappearing into the shadows around the side of the building, but his flaring cigarette cherry betrays him. "Wish somebody'd told me we were doing a record cover because I would've had my hair cut first," he mutters.

Anton's hair is freshly cut to *Meet the Beatles* Ringo specs, that being full but slightly tight around the edges, while Matt's seems to have gone pudding dessert bowl.

"Matt, don't you want to be on the cover of the record you play on?" he asks coaxingly.

Matt takes off his glasses, squints, shakes his hair out, and then pats it down again. Anton depresses the camera button, and out comes a depressed but workable shot of Matt.

Pleased with the results so far, he looks over at me, smiling with his own subliminal eye flash. They are very bright, especially when conducting a band basic training inspection. Most of us were beyond this need and hence why we were here in the first place, but still there were

9

certain criteria to be met, such as complying with this being an unspoken "no beards allowed" zone. If you ever found yourself past the three-day stubble mark, a disposable razor would magically appear from a parka pocket. "Don't you want to shave? Here."

Again the palpable intent, this time a look within a look that I wasn't sure meant I was doing good in all of this or just good for doing. It's become such a familiar look and yet one I'm still trying to figure out.

"Okay, Joel, you're last, c'mon."

As much as I was dying to be on an album cover for the first time, Dean and I weren't even around yet for the recording of this album. Still, I eagerly strike a pose, and he full-blows another flash off, this time straight in my face and totally blinding me. I never did find out how many licks it takes to get to the center of a Tootsie Pop, but I can tell you it takes eleven blinks for a nighttime camera light flash show to jump around into complete nonexistence.

"Nope. This won't work; looks like you're not on the cover."

He hands me the picture, then turns the camera on himself, poses, and takes the last shot.

I didn't think it was such a bad picture of me really, especially after Anton returned from Bomp! Records owner Greg Shaw's house with the final design and I saw how obscured the other four faces turned out. In the end, there would be another random Polaroid coming soon that would get me an album cover all to myself, but for now, I couldn't help but feel frustrated. Dean wasn't actually on the record either, but now his face was going to be on the cover, and I was in the band before he was! This was my internal setup when Anton asked me to take care of an errand for him while he was away.

"Here, go with Dave D to drop this picture off for the new seven-inch single cover. Mike has all the type info already; he just needs this." He hands me a small black-and-white photo of a couple making disturbingly happy-looking faces in a small claustrophobic-looking 1970s suburban living room.

"It's Brian Glaze's parents. It'll be weird."

"Cool," I agree. It did have a sort of Smiths record cover vibe, in that it was ordinary human subjects in a black-and-white slice of everyday life from another era. Stilll … wouldn't it be cool, I thought, if the whole current BJM line up was on the cover?

"*Suure*," our manager, Dave D, replies next to me the very next day from the driver's seat of his parents' new Lexus. Even in his enthusiasm, I could tell that it was less about my idea being a good one and more about him enjoying the idea of me going directly against Anton's wishes for the cover art for what was to be the "Anemone"/"Cold to the Touch" double A-side vinyl single.

"C'mon, we'll stop by my place so you can go through my huge box of band photos and pick out some cool ones."

"You don't think he'll be pissed?"

"Nah, man … not if it looks cool, and how can a

picture collage of all you guys not look cool?" he adds in band-managerial positive reinforcement of me going against Anton's plan.

Every gig since the band's beginning, Dave D not only filmed every set on his video camera but also provided a still camera or two for friends and associates to take photos for him. I open Dave D's giant box of photos and am grateful to see that the most recent ones of our now-current lineup are floating around the top of the huge photo paper mass that dated all the way back to the first Peacock Lounge show.

I make my cover collage mock-up right there sitting on his bed, starting clockwise from the top; a bass-playing Matt; next a shot of Mara on stage singing "Anemone"; under her Brian and Dean backstage drinking; then Jeff and Anton sharing a guitar moment; and then rounding out the display right at the ten o'clock position is yours truly with trusty tambourine in hand. Then, I take the photo of Brian's parents Anton intended to be the entire cover image and plop it diagonally in the center of my band arrangement.

"Oh … okay, so you want *all* of these on there?" Candy Floss Record's owner, Mike Toi, asks when we show him my design at his rented office record label space in the heart of the Financial District.

I'd gotten myself onto a record cover, but it didn't look very good.

To make up for this, the following week, I show up to our next gig for load-in earlier than the rest of the band. When I arrive at the Trocadero Transfer in the SoMa District, he is already outside grinning from ear to ear from the back of our manager Dave D's van. At the van's open rear doors is a Hammond B3, which is basically a church organ, with double-tiered keyboards and a row of large foot pedals all housed in thick lacquered mahogany. It's quite a large piece of musical furniture that's really only meant to be moved once, that being from the music store showroom floor to its permanent studio or side-of-pulpit living spot.

Slightly confused in that *I hope this isn't what it looks like* fashion, I'm still eager to please in order to rectify my record cover blunder, and even though he hasn't really given me a hard time about it, I could tell he had been disappointed, a moment that instantaneously made me realize my design choices did indeed ruin the cover.

We lift the beyond-heavy organ out of the van and lug the thing through the doors of the venue where, once inside, the full reality of the situation hits. This isn't simply a situation of lifting this the rest of the way to the stage about ten yards away, but up the curved stairs lining the far wall, leading high up to the venue's second and much smaller room. Accessing the climb from way down here, the high winding slope of carpeted stairs looks to grow even steeper as they get toward the top of its fifty-odd-step summit. Its black carpet's green, purple, yellow, and pink eighties swirl patterns look like organized candy regurgitation, while high at the top, this technicolor yawn takes on a twinkling tacky-twilight effect against the large all-black club interior.

I give the upright-piano-sized Hammond B3 organ one last look and sigh before Anton and I would be starting up the first step. Already gripping the organ again from the first step, Anton pulls slow and hard as I tense up and hesitate, "Are we really doing this?" I want to ask but don't.

"Yes," he says in response to my narcing facial expression. "Ready? Lift!"

I quickly push up on the lip of the cabinet top with my palms, raising my end, while his lift from a step up tilts the organ diagonally toward me, and we grunt it up twelve steps. He sets down his end on the current highest step and quickly runs down to my firmly shaking side of the organ to help me keep it anchored up at a horizontal dangle.

Now taking a moment to look around for possible help, I can see all the venue crew, security, and other staff milling about in what I suppose is getting everything prepared for tonight's industrial music dance night going on in this main room. Whatever tasks they are into now, no matter how small, they are all seemingly suddenly too busy to help the upstairs small room local act huff their massively heavy piece of gear up the steps.

"Okay, we can do this—ready? Hold it up now. You're doing great!" Anton says now in a motivating personal trainer tone as he runs back to the top end.

We heave-ho once again, and it whines a Dracula's coffin impersonation as we step-by-step take it for another seven. Now that we are past the halfway point, it's far longer than it had looked from the bottom. I brace myself and again help him hold the organ straight. Its creakings and croakings have been getting progressively wearier, as if questioning even its own willingness to continue the journey. How did I wind up here on this new wave/abstract decorated escalator currently moving me higher toward my probable downward demise into a funeral-pyre pile of splintered wood and piano keys? All muscles clenched, I loom over the ridge of the banister and down its vertical wall. Vertigo begins weaving knots in my stomach, and I close my eyes. Any and all chances to retreat back down the stairs with the organ are long gone. We would have to force our way to the top no matter what. It's all going painfully slow and getting progressively darker the higher we go. All the upper-level lights are off, adding to the isolated feeling that the two of us are completely alone up here. I gaze between my extended arms all the way down the sweeping slope below.

By now, we've made it close enough to the top of the stairs that the venue staff feels it's safe to come out from hiding and start setting up our small stage without having to help us with our instrument-moving. We grunt it up to the top and back onto flat land like rescuing a majestic mountain bison from being stuck on a high ridge.

It turns out that the player of the Hammond B3 organ that night, the one we'd dragged all the way up those stairs, is just a matchbook that Anton stuck between two keys to hold down a single droning "A" note throughout the entire set. The note was only ever a single note but still one of mystic sixties incantation, of the like used to conjure ancient magic spells such as "Time of the Season" and "Whiter Shade of Pale." A red-and-green electric sonic wave that never crashes on any shore as hounds-toothed and striped sailors set the sails and cast off onto its revolving timeless drift.

Helping Anton move a mountain so that a single

15

butterfly might live on it is just the type of cause I was living for. That intense do-or-die spirit fueled the sound and songs, and I was there to learn from it and to augment it with my own character in any way I could. Still, all that being said, I still had no intention of helping load band gear ever again. When the gig is over, with tambourine and maracas in hand, I put my toes on tippy and jingle back down those stairs as quietly as I can.

Daze in the Life

"Heyyy, what's the address saay on that flyer?" Dave D asks with his regular extended-length Cali drawl tightened to promote a timely answer.

"1757 Pomona," I read from my lap. This is my favorite BJM flyer so far, featuring Brian Jones pulling a face with his pinky pulling out a nostril from the inside, or a "nanker" as he'd called it. Apparently, it was something all the Stones did among themselves to keep spirits up during the lean pre-fame days, and seeing as we arc in Davis, which is practically Sacramento, I can't just go collect another one off a Haight Street telephone pole like I'd done more than once before, so I'm keeping this one close.

"Seventeeen fifty-seven Poe-moe-nuuuuhhh ... all riiight ... there it is!"

Anton, Brian, Dean, and Matt are in the rest of the seats of Dave's first van, which for the time being enables these quick-shot single gigs around the bay and other points beyond like here in Davis.

We pull off the street in this very family-friendly neighborhood and onto the long, flat driveway of a 1950s-looking townhouse. "We're playing *here?*" Dean scoffs.

"Yep," Dave confirms with amusement, then adds with ironic endearment, "This is a symbol of how big you guys are right now at this moment." He scans the room for acknowledgments, but we're all too busy doing our *Bad News Bears* team-style synchronized gape-mouthed routine. Returning to managerial seriousness, he then assures, "Don't worry, the guy putting this on says this place will be packed tonight."

"Let's see if we can set up," Anton says with a flip of the hair and a swish of a parka sleeve as he pushes the passenger's-side door open. Time to get into it.

I slide the side door open and step down and into stride formation behind Anton in my newly acquired secondhand square-toe leather zip-boots, tight double-dyed black jeans, a black-and-red *Get Carter* ringer T, and my cafe racer-style leather jacket. Matt's bob-mop fops as he high-steps down and quickens to my side in brown single-buckle shoes, black Sta-Prest Levi's, and matching silver pearl western button-up. Despite the cold, he has no jacket on, for some reason. Behind us, Dean struts casual in low winklepickers, black stovepipes, and is wrapped in a long velvet peacoat with a silver paisley ascot tucked in neat. His blond hair is shorter after getting it cut yesterday, but even more so than usual after such an event.

Brian coolly gangles behind in his way, blond hair product-pushed back with a vintage red flannel Pendleton jacket, Converse, and blue jeans. There is something about him that suggests *Catcher in the Rye* going to the San Francisco Art Academy. Here comes Jeff in a twee skip-up next to Dean. He wears slim pinstripe suit trousers, a little-boy-looking knit seventies Munich Olympics–type sweater with sunglasses pushed up into the face of his puffy pinned-at-the back pompadour. Dave is in his everyday uniform of Docs, black 501s, and leather

18

motorcycle jacket, and his longer-than-the-rest-of-us legs
get him to the door right after Anton, to which he
graciously herds the rest of us in with an arm extended.

Once in, it's back out as I weirdly begin to help
unload gear, but by my second-lightest available load,
Anton has established new house rule, meaning now I'll
just hang back casually as one of the visiting dignitaries
from the San Francisco music scene. As the rest begin to
set up in the modest-size living room, the suburban man-
boys move away the furniture. I am reminded of that
scene in *Pulp Fiction* with the suitcase and the frat kids,
but instead of "Hey, Flock of Seagulls," it would be "Hey,
Inspiral Carpets."

Cords are uncoiled and foot pedals are plugged into
Fender Twin Reverb amps, followed by instrument tuning
into chord play that forms progressions, and the large
empty A-frame living room space begins to take the
reverb in whole. Matt gets a bass sound booming as Brian
casually turns a snare drum key, while I, in my infinite
daze, have forgotten that at the last show, I'd broken my
one good tambourine into pieces before stomping my
maracas into a pile of dusty ornate broken eggshells
during a jacked-up speed bender huff. It made perfect
sense at the time. I mean, it must have, especially when I
speculate my awareness of my total lack of funds for new
replacements, but those people were just not *getting* it, and
something had to be done, seemingly.

Two hours later, with a case of beer down and a
couple bottle passes round in our green room van, it's time
to play. The predictions were good, and the place is in fact
booming in numbers as I grab my small back-up junker

tambourine with only four cymbals and we hit the corner of the living room. Even with no stage, to me this area is even more so where Anton is like no other in otherworldliness by way of performance and song. He delivers the vocal goods with casual intensity, soulful and full of before-his-age life experiences. From behind my bubble shades, I sideways watch his scheme of spun sensations run with full-on emotion emulsion emoting in thick vocal fortitude while guitar ramble-tambling through the oncoming grooves.

Everything is being set in place for the big push. It's time to prepare to go undercover and infiltrate the Man. To transcend to the next level and disrupt the system from the inside. To do this properly, all us current BJM ducks need some, well, *any* order, especially me. BJM had by now bagged two of the four diversely inspired albums that will come out next year, and it's getting rightfully time to get tired of all the local BS attitude and general nonacceptance from our home town of San Francisco. Song after song, we receive extra enthusiasm that comes from places outside of big city–style competitiveness. They appreciate the effort and are not afraid to give it back to us. *They* get it, and this is all a sign of greater things to come.

Greater things like where my favorite band The Verve's career was, whom I'm going to see live the very next night at Slim's. I'd seen them there last year on their first tour over from the UK for the album *A Storm in Heaven*, but by this time they've gone up another career level and are busting off extra dates anytime they have a break from the current Lollapalooza tour. Since the I-Beam closed down over on Haight Street, Slim's in the SOMA District has become *the* place in San Francisco where all the new British bands now played. Just in the last few months, I'd seen Slowdive, RIDE, My Bloody Valentine, The Charlatans, and Primal Scream all at Slim's.

With only three instruments and a charismatic vocalist, The Verve had the rare artistic gift of being able to transport a listener to outer sonic worlds that did not previously exist. When I'd enthusiastically played Anton the track "A Man Called Sun," he, in his typical impossible-to-impress fashion, dismissed them by observing that "this guy sounds like Bono."

Having come straight to the live venue from work, I'm early. I enter the club and expect to be bored, but that's when I see up in the high side-of-stage DJ perch is singer Richard Ashcroft, spinning records unannounced. I walk into the middle of the sparsely populated floor as Curtis Mayfield's classic "The Pusherman" grooves on. I look up. He looks down, sees me, and gives me the solidarity fist. I salute back, and all is right in the universe.

The tune ends, and he disappears while the local whatever Who Cares and the Gang band start preparing to open up the show. I head downstairs to the men's room, and just as I eye the first stall, Chris comes out of it. "Heyy, man," he says, smiling wide, then downshifts and draws out casual, "Dude, *sniff*, I gotta bounce. There's a new chick I'm meeting outside, but hey, try one of these E's out." Then he snaps to attention. "Pretty good shit."

Back upstairs, I wait with anticipation for the E to come on. The first band finishes, and it hasn't come on yet. The gear switchover happens, and still nothing. The Verve come out with full grooves a-blazing from the opener "Slide Away" and all the way through to the set closer "Feel"; still nothing. Nothing? Man, Chris always has the best of everything. The band is leaving the stage, and I look around the room in case I can spot my ecstasy high floating around somewhere. That's when I see, elevated above the crowd, my friend Omar, who weirdly is being allowed to use the large antique mahogany bar as seating. This privilege is a clear indication the night is over and another display of how connected he is through being one of the founding DJs of our San Francisco Britpop Headquarters, Popscene. I push through and hike myself up. "Omar, I can't believe they didn't do 'Gravity Grave!'"

"Don't worry, man, they're gonna do it." As if on cue, the band returns to the stage and as promised the ultra-vibey bass line of "Gravity Grave" begins its rolling, extraterrestrial traveler's groove over, around and up into every crevice in the room.

Suddenly, and out of nowhere, the E hits me full swing, launching me in its chemical ejector seat, as I'm now rocketing in my best *Voyager 1* impersonation going from zero to 18,000 miles per hour. I break orbit just in time for the vocals.

Get back get back again and again...

Bang a Bong

It was this sort of behavior that soon had me suddenly with no place of employment, which then tipped the second domino in line(s) that was losing permanent residence San Francisco. Luckily, at the time, I still had couches to alternate, but I'd be quick to wear those cushions out if I went pro charity case.

Then, as if the employment agency-in-the-sky looked down and smiled, the position of "Flyer Person" opened up where Matt Hollywood worked at Escape from New York Pizza. Their flyer person's job consisted of one thing and one thing only, standing on the corner of Haight and Cole Streets, handing out a pizza coupon flyer to every passer-by. Further groovin' the simplicity of the gig was that the hours were a mere 11 a.m. to 1 p.m. Two hours, two days a week, and with free lunch, and I didn't have to be there until late morning. *Surely*, I couldn't fuck that up.

Four days a week, you could find Matt standing behind this pizza-slice counter with face pursed in defiance, slinging slices with scoffing disdain at any and all who entered sans girly cuteness asking for sizzling wares, which is by all appearances his only available retaliation against the pizza-enjoying sect of society who'd been given the power to slowly torture him to death. I'd been eating here a lot more often lately anyway, as he would hook my penniless fanny up with the unsold end of the night-hardened slabs, but as it was my first day of employment here, today was my first time breaching the cramped serving counter and kitchen space to the back office. As it always seems to be, Matt's got a line going out the door and looks pretty pissed off to be alive at this moment, so I don't stop to chat while also collecting white clouds of free-flowing flour onto my black stitches.

In the back office, sitting at his desk, is the owner of Escape from New York, Joe Goldmark. Originally from New York and anciently in his late forties, he seemingly has a condition to forever act and react in slow motion, and his permanent unhurriedness unconsciously lords over all velocity terms of conversation flow. He, being the purse-string prospect, this was an incredibly formidable power to the composure of a speed freak. Joe was also an aspiring bluegrass pedal steel star back in the seventies and eighties, but by now has been resigned to local yokel happy hour detail around town.

"Hrrr yuh go," he dude-ranch-with-a-Jewish-deli delivers while handing me two stacks of handbill flyers, both identical, but one stack red and the other lime colored. He then drone-drawls long as if Sam Elliott were the schoolteacher for the Peanuts gang, "Go down to the corner of Haight and Cole and hand 'em out to every single person that walks by."

"Got it," I assure him, and off I go.

These mid-nineties days on a sunny Haight Street morning, it could still be like a Peter Max rainbow world of full clear blue with partly puffies on down to the anonymous grid of fairytale-like Vics and Eds, stilted yet prancy in the parade they make, when this being just after

24

eleven, it was still well within the early no-aggo time zone before the street punks got too drunk and surly and the homeless got too hungry and started getting overly aggressive with their sparing-of-change requests. By now, this form of change has long held dominance over the other airborne one from the sixties.

I walk the block down to my designated corner and commence working on my flyer style. Not wanting to seem too eager, I do a sort of meet me halfway handout, kinda like I do on stage, unless somebody cute or cool looking walks by; then I try to throw a little subtle personality into my handoff form.

Periodically I'm seeing friends cruise by whom I think are interesting or bullshit on depending scales. About an hour into it, Mara walks by and smiles in humored shock that I'm employed in any capacity whatsoever. I bow and extend a flyer as if it's a royal item of worth. Mara is one of the best combinations of down-to-earth and cool I've ever known, and it's no wonder the song "Anemone" involved her input.

This is the final stamp of approval for me, and as she continues on, I whisper under my breath, "This is going to work." Because I didn't want to have a job, I wanted to be in a band. The Velvet Underground never had jobs. Primal Scream never had jobs. I was going to do it for real and not have a job either.

Anyway, this isn't really work, this is standing around, which I would have been doing anyway. Standing here in this spot for a few hours would net me about twenty dollars a day to live on. But the fact that I think for even a moment that I'm going to keep any kind of budget going and not burn through my wages in two days tops proves that I'm still not all business. The dreamer inside still remains intact.

Then I get spotted by Manny, a rave party promoter who recognizes me from his big warehouse party BJM had played recently along the abandoned dock area. Manny has a shaved head and is a bit girthy, but not the intimidating model, yet still with that all-business smolder of a late-night club scene-maker who puts on events where lots of known illegal drugs are definitely being taken.

Seeing that in addition to my late-night tambourine skills I'm also a professional daytime flyer-er, he also offers me a gig to hand advertise for his new techno night at the DNA Lounge. It was becoming apparent to all the party people that—like what would eventually happen with weed—it was sadly time to come above ground and make it legal. The fuzz was just starting to grow too thick, and for party promoters, making a lot more money off the metamorphosis won't be all that bad a side effect. At least until the adverse effects settle in, causing premature music scene death, but maybe that won't happen this time.

Now things are really looking up! I'm high on getting it together after having started to totally depend on "the kindness of others" like an American Britpop Blanche DuBois or something. I finish out my hours for the day, punch the clock, and get paid my Alexander Hamilton twins.

Surely, I can celebrate a little this first day, plus it's an opportunity to keep things copacetic with the living-room-couch suite at Chez Matt. I treat us to sniffs and a round at Dylan's Irish Pub and Bay Area scooter mod magnet, which is conveniently located downstairs from his second-floor apartment.

Later, letting the eye-level streetlamps outside and the television do the lighting, we leave the sound off, to leave as little risk as possible of alerting his roommates behind closed bedroom doors that there is a two-man party now in progress. Bizarrely, the opening credits to the film *Seconds* is on the TV screen, with its eyeballs and mouths in extreme and distorted black-and-white close-ups as we each get our facefuls. Then, we each collect an acoustic guitar and move it into the kitchen. Being totally jacked up, we—in an effort to tweak stealthily—are barely making contact with the strings but yet are strumming at a hundred miles an hour and on and on and on while Matt whispers intensely hushed words and my jaw breakdances in pop locks and rotations.

... *zhang zhang zhang zhangzhangzhang zhang zhang zhang zhangzhangzhang zhang zhang zhang* ...

Hours later, I snap out of the trance and ask, "Matt, what are we doing?"

"I dunno."

We were on this record-skipping groove for I don't know how long and had both turned glazy and reddish with time, and now the sun is starting to add blue anti-Nosferatu twilight to the electric yellow refracting off the white walls. I'm tingling all over, and suddenly we hear the sound of the bathroom door being opened and closed down the hall. Normal people are about to start their day! We exchange a surprised wordless glance and quickly high-step tippy-toe into his bedroom to hide.

A few hours later, I say good night to Matt, who's

planning on sleeping off his day off before our BJM gig at the Purple Onion tonight. I've blown all my cash from the day before and walk the one-hour distance to my second flyer shift. At this stage in my life, I'd watched the sun come up while buzzing somewhere outdoors at least a hundred times. I'm sure that must have some sort of permanent effect that can't be all bad, if not in fact quite the opposite. The "hooker with a heart of gold" of drug effects on the mind.

Maybe I'm just strung out—well, I *am* strung out, but still, today seems to be one of those days every couple of months when the old Saint Joseph's Hospital over on the other side of Buena Vista Park has some sort of out-day program for the mental health patients who lived there in a type of assisted-living situation. Mostly people from wealthy families who couldn't or didn't want to deal with their special care needs. It was a kooky addition to the Haight Street thing, an already kooky place and most welcome.

Always occurring earlier in the day, the out-day wanderers would be window shopping in singles and pairs and very much seemed to be enjoying themselves in a similar way to the day-old Deadheads, coming in and out of shops and stopping at window displays to have extra-long visual conversations with window displays that spoke to them. Back at my last-ever "real" job at Reckless Records, it was just this semi-regular seemingly random occurrence on Haight Street that colored up the faded, washed-too-many-times tie-dyed streets for a couple of hours.

I'm flyering with much more reserve today, despite

feeling better than I should. (I have a weird condition where I enjoy being strung out—that up all night and not high anymore but residually not tired lucidness.) I see, walking my way, a long, thin Latino man with long and thin everything else, smiling to himself in an amused and surprised yet knowing way. He gives me a nod as he passes, as if granting me some unspoken permission, and I return-pose for him as if I were one of the Jesus characters in a church stained-glass window, perhaps herding a single baby sheep while one foot is placed atop a snake. My arm is bent slightly at the elbow, with thumb and middle fingertips touching, pinky and index out and head slightly tilted just so.

Across the street, a young Black girl wearing Coke-bottle-lens glasses is with a short balloon boy sporting a caterpillar mustache and walking on tippy-toes. They stop and take in every shop window on this adventure together, two explorers traveling through the customary eleven o'clock opening-time quiet, seeming genuinely unburdened. Traditionally, it's a pretty cute day.

Then someone I recognize is coming toward me down on the shoulder of the hippie highway. It's Paola, who'd sung a song with Anton on *Methadrone*. I've also heard recently that she was really into Wiccan witchcraft or something. When I inquire as to possible demon talent agency dealings, she's a bit taken aback, followed by adamantly downplaying the possibilities, which for me actually gives her some legitimacy, being that the witchy thing wasn't just an identity act to seem more interesting to people. She certainly had a good look for it, always dressed black dominant, small in frame with dark hair over dark ringed Keane-esque "big eyes." What I'm suddenly thinking is, in tangent with wanting to inspire her to reach for the black stars, is maybe she can at least discover the inner power to, through incantation, summon an "other" to this realm where I can then try to BS my way into a "Sympathy for the Devil" type of deal.

Underneath her slightly intrigued unwillingness, I can tell by her shyer-than-standard state, yet still tinged with almost-hidden amusement, that she is in fact entertained by the thought of this Satanic Majesties' request. Ultimately, she turns me down, but at least somebody around here knows how far I'm willing to go with whatever it is.

Paola continues down Cole Street toward the Panhandle Park, where incidentally the "Human Be-in" concert and general all-purpose hippie hang session had kicked off "The Summer of Love," and I watch her walk away for a few moments, still lingering on the dark possibilities. I turn back around, and it's about halfway to home along my neck-twist journey that I see what looks to be a pitch-black hole wearing a top hat, floating down the sidewalk in my direction. It gets closer, and I'm starting to think maybe it's a person wearing an overcoat or maybe a Victorian-style coach driver's type of cape, but it's all blur-blobbed together in its hole-in-reality-ness.

The hole is up close now, and after such a float approach, I can't help but stare in my strung-outness, almost as if hypnotized to do so. There is a crease in the hole, and through it an off-white opaque face glistens like a sea creature, peeking through a long, black, stringy hair curtain that disappears into and furthers the blob-black ink spot top-hat-topped appearance. The one very discernible feature, at least to me, is all the white tiny skin bumps from eyelid to brow, like ribbed but randomly, and that somehow seemed to physically represent the power of whatever it was—like they were the members of the board calling the shots, which were thankfully far beyond my understanding.

These types of out-of-nowhere aberrations are the stuff of things that can shatter a fragile eggshell comedown mind, and not realizing that I'm staring—which isn't cool to do, regardless of why and whatever, something I'd spent a few years on the other side of while having my adolescence force-spent in a redneck town. Those, to me, were simple post-punk stylings of ratted-up hair and maybe some thin eyeliner to make for slight flirtations with androgyny; to them, it was full hardcore drag. I quickly turn away to find hands to hand flyers to, not recognizing that the best thing I could have just done is give the hole a flyer, to conclude our already rocky relationship. Alas, as it is, my strung-out scatter-brained snub has been cast.

I pass out flyers to the passers-by, suddenly eager to do so like nothing is going on out of the ordinary, other than my level of enthusiasm to be handing out flyers, waiting for the hole to appear in my side view while continuing on to a hole's hang spot, but no, the Hole has just set up camp about six feet behind me, now squatting and creating a hole in the sidewalk, which he's still poking up halfway through while starting to mumble a low, rumble-chilling chant where the words have no spaces between them, nor even seem to have beginning or endings. A mantra spoken in a drone made of only middle symbols, or to call it what it was, weird.

I turn to the Hole and glare in defiance, to generate some sort of "shoo" beam from my eyes, but this just consummates the dance I now have going with this much older person. At twenty-four and twenty thousand leagues out of my depth here, there is suddenly only one thing and one thing only for sure, and that is I no longer have the desire to do this job. As impossible as it sounds, it's as if I've just been stripped of my enthusiasm for all things flyers, and I realize I must have just been cursed.

Still, I do want to get paid, so I have to finish out the remaining half-hour of the shift to the tune of the mantra-mumbles. It's a free country, and I can't tell holes in time and space visiting from other dimensional whereabouts where they can and can't curse people.

Whatever this case may be, maybe you can tell me, because I'm suddenly coming down way too hard and fast. What I do know of my current situation, I'm pretty sure, is that a strung-out, know-nothing twenty-something with probably a lot more hyphen-inducing properties than that young person has black magic wish-opened a portal to another dimension, and as a result, a Hole has escaped and seemingly cursed me to never have the willpower to be employed again.

I get paid and leave Haight Street that day, knowing that I still have the Manny windshield wiper disbursement job waiting, which I can at least do in a state of mobility. This, I reckon, will be much safer than just standing on a corner collecting curses all day. The confirmation in the curse comes the next day, when I get the DNA flyers off

Manny at his apartment, which is also just off the Panhandle. I take the flyers and walk the couple of blocks up to Haight Street, where I start clipping them under windshield wipers along Buena Vista Park. By the time I make a meager few blocks to Central Street, it's perfectly clear I no longer have the power to conjure the ambition to continue with this. The old me, who could whip flyers out, is dead, and as it is, the curse has worked, and now I can't work. I was cursed!

Then I see Michelle from my old Reckless job crossing the street ahead, probably heading there right now. She was always a rock of responsibility, and the sight of her on her way to display her care wares there inspires me to tap into my old responsible self, but it's no good, for he is dead now. I throw the remaining flyers into the next trash can I see, where Manny will find them later while combing my assigned route after I fail to show back up at his apartment.

Handing out flyers was the lowest I could go and still be doing something employee-ish before flatlining. The faint blip on the heart monitor is slowing ... slowing ... *beeeeeeeee* ...

... ONG!

BONG!

BONG! I'm suddenly conscious from inside orange-lit eyelids and with a circus elephant balancing on my head by one leg. I slowly, painfully open my eyes to a sideways world. It's a bright, cold, wet one and covered with cement, which the side of my face is currently planted into. A small boy halfway up the steps only visible to me from the waist up points and exclaims, "Mommy, why is that person laying down there? Is he hurt?"

"No, honey, he just has no home to sleep in," his mother answers, frosting a thin layer of sympathy over her annoyance while clutching tighter to his other hand.

BONG!

I look up. Rising high above me is a church bell tower. I peel my squinty head off the ground and look around me to find its "off" button. It appears the morning church congregation is arriving for Sunday Mass, and I'm sleeping in front of its giant glass doors. I awkwardly animate up from the concrete like one of the *Jason and the Argonauts* skeletons and hobble down the steps, passing through the mutters, cold looks, and shaking heads.

From the bottom of the St. Ignatius Church steps, I start down Fulton Street, and once familiarity begins to cut through the fog, I soon realize that if I keep going this way, I could be at Dean Taylor's apartment in about another ten minutes. While my body is moistly covered in the morning dew, my insides feel as dry as a box wine bag sucked empty, which is basically exactly what they are. I put one hand to my stomach and with the other wipe the tiny implanted pebbles from my face along with the other debris, when suddenly I catch a glimpse of my reflection in a parked car window.

It appears that the dew moisture mixed with the hairspray job I'd applied to my mod-goth rat's-nest hairdo has reformed and hardened the street side into a flat wall spanning from the top of my ear straight up six inches high above my head. You could hold a carpenter's level tool against it and get a perfectly straight reading. I then, in further painful examination, turn this "Flock of Seagulls" half of my head to the side and see that the flattened surface has the texture of just-dumped canned spaghetti that refuses to move. More tiny pebbles, leaves, and debris are embedded within the wall, making for a fossil-like world frozen in time. In some futile attempt to fix myself up, I pull a few of the individual stalks outward, each resisting the journey and quickly bouncing back like old, rusty bedsprings. I continue working at it, and after walking past a few more cars, I check my reflection again and see I've managed to coax a few to stick out like twisted cypress trees growing from the coastal cliffs.

As I continue on my death march, the timing of my Cuban heels on the wet pavement reminds me of the cowbell from The Chambers Brothers' psychedelic soul classic "Time Has Come Today." The lyrics could not have been more poignant—

I have no place to stay ...

I walk in time with the cowbell until I make it to the old house of Kenneth Anger, who among many outsider things was once a brief Satanic adviser to The Rolling Stones. Named "The Westerfeld House," it's an old Victorian whose dark decorative architecture makes it look like the case study house for *The Addams Family*. This is where he would have lived when the Stones first met him.

I continue on, and just a half block further down, I make it to Dean's. I give the brass ring door knocker three hopeful whacks and wait. No answer. After a few forever

35

moments, I turn around and notice the row of "Painted Ladies" houses are over on the opposite side of the park. One of those famous postcard-picturesque Edwardian homes must be empty now that the stupid *Full House* show has been canceled, I thought. Maybe I could brea—

Suddenly, the door swings open behind me, and there is Dean in a burgundy silk robe with matching pajamas. He gives me a good once over. "Huh-huh-ho! What happened to you, buddy?" he chuckles.

I am so relieved he is home that his amusement at my latest foray into buffoonery is weirdly comforting.

"It's a long story, but the last thing I remember is me and Matt getting into an argument late last night, and I walked off drunk and passed out on some church steps. We were drinking whiskey at a party nearby, and he just lost it because he says, "I never listen to him.""

"Man, who does?" he jokes, and as I chuckle back, the big picture presents itself to him as to why I was on his doorstep at ten after nine on a Sunday morning. "So, he kicked you out, huh?"

"I kinda kicked myself out."

"Well, jeez man, you look like crap!" he says playfully, then feigning an authoritative tone, "C'mon, you can come crash on the couch. Christina's in the shower. I'll tell her what's up."

"Thanks, man," I reply, feeling more grateful than any time I could currently remember.

He smiles a friendly got-your-back smile. "Yeahh, don't worry—I gotcha ... loser."

Where I Was while They Were Getting High

I decided it couldn't just be an audio hallucination due to the LSD. From off in the distance, I was hearing what sounded like some sort of giant escaped animal's mating call, or even more frightening, the hunting horns gorilla soldiers blew while herding wild humans in the original *Planet of the Apes*. Actually, for me, in the mid-nineties, seeing these types of things would almost seem possible.

Only a few moments ago, I had ventured off the main road that runs through Golden Gate Park and into "the wilderness." I was now away from the concrete jungle of San Francisco and frolicking in pigeon-toed orange-peel abandon as my own private space nature commander. I'd been on this trip enough times to know that environment is everything, so I'd staged my happening on the original playground of the Summer of Love, tripping at a level worthy of the grand traditions of these sacred lands.

Hidden away within the mass of bushes and trees, I held a leaf and examined its veins. They pulsed within it, and as I watched further, they began to spread out and into my own hand. I did recognize this as an electric cliché, but still, I truly did feel connected with the entire universe through my little leaf conduit. I was safe, at least for the rest of daylight, when then the effects of the LSD would start wearing off.

The night before had begun with The Brian

Jonestown Massacre performing at Slim's, followed by a little after party at Anton's newly acquired shared apartment. In addition to Matt and Dean's, I'd also begun crashing there from time to time and currently crushing out on a girl who, after enough drinks to know better, talked me into dropping acid with her. This was at 4 a.m.

We had only enough time to seal our trip pact with paper to tongue before she was abruptly dragged off by her apparent chaperone and our apparent band manager Dave D, who had been turning progressively grumpier. The forty-five-minute ride back down the highway home to Palo Alto was held over her head and she reluctantly gave in. Subsequently, the move then succeeded in tipping the rest of the party dominos, and within minutes I was alone sitting in the soon-to-be-living living room.

The inevitably of Anton and his roommates waking up to find me sitting there peaking with all heads on deck had me quickly going over my escape options. Golden Gate Park made the most sense for someone in my position, and I calculated that if I left immediately, I could walk from where I was now in SOMA and get up to the park in about thirty minutes before I started to trip the light fantastic. With a mile and a half of vast nature to hide in, what could go wrong?

The wailing calls got louder and nearer. What was happening? Why was it happening? *Was* it happening?

All I could feel for certain was that it certainly wasn't a "happening" as the very un-groovy bellows got closer and louder still. So close now, I could no longer ignore whatever the impending invasion was. I crept back up to the road's edge, remaining hidden behind the thick brush.

As the ever-increasing loudness grew, other noises were revealed and morphed into a swirling soundscape mixing into 500.1 3-D audio channeling into the mixing board of my mind with all knobs twiddling. Rising low rumbles of many drums banging out of sync with high-pitched whistles clattering atop like rain on a hot tin hangar roof.

It was the rising sounds of absolute chaos, and they were coming for me. I spread the bushes apart slowly and turned my head sideways to peer down the road. My kaleidoscope eyes bloomed beyond their sockets, while my mouth spiraled into a vortex of terror.

In the distance, I saw an army of thousands upon thousands of marathon runners in a swirling mass of forward motion, lumbering straight towards me. The 1997 Bay to Breakers Marathon was in full swing, an annual footrace over 100,000 strong with a course that runs straight through the center of Golden Gate Park.

Not just a massive, celebrated footrace for serious runners but also a day for additional thousands of normal people to wave their freak flags that only come out this once a year.

Here they all came, wearing their red numbered flags: the ugly naked people, a pink gorilla, a port-a-potty wearing sneakers, comic book superheroes of questionable physical authenticity, a giant human centipede, a monk, the Grim Reaper, British Redcoats, jocks blowing stadium horns and rolling beer keg carts, botched body paint jobs, a fat suit man, a half-Elvis/half-dude bro, Ronald Reagan, unintentional Huey Lewis lookalikes, ninjas, a human head atop a bunch of grapes that could run, and on and on.

The head of the nightmare was now almost right in

39

front of me, a running and sweating and bulging mass getting closer and closer and louder and louder.

With the noise now at ear-splitting, mind-bending pitch, I recoiled back in terror into my now-peaceless shire, stumbling back up against a tree. I watched through the brush as the gigantic lame-wave began to spill past. The whole park had been instantly flash-flooded like a massive "normo" dam broke.

With leaves stuck to my back and twigs in my hair, I retreated backward through the brush, out of the side of the park onto Fulton Street. I was cast out of my Eden, in more ways than one.

* * * *

The one and only time Anton and I had gotten into it physically one-on-one came just a few nights later, when he and I were drinking whiskey on his shared apartment living room couch and I began dissing on Matt a little, for whatever reason, which is usually just trying to be funny in ways I think people will like. For some new unforeseen reason, this caused a completely unexpected snap reaction out of Anton, and suddenly I found myself running down the two flights of outdoor apartment building stairs and into the street, where my suitcase had finally stopped bouncing down. Now in a rage, I began yelling back up at him and causing a scene. He came down. We fist-fought right there in the gutter as Mara and his girlfriend Dawn came down and watched on. It's okay, people fight sometimes. Especially drunk people, and after having once rolled around a New Mexico parking lot with Matt, this suddenly and unexpectedly becomes my second real one, other than just getting group-pounced by jocks and rednecks in high school.

He "won," and probably would have anyway, even had I not, after some sidewalk wrestling, stopped fighting back and let him hit me in the face over and over again. All the while, I was glaring back at him in hard passiveness, waiting for him to want to stop—which took quite a few more than I'd planned on when flash-instigating this plan. In a weird way, this made me the winner—that is, if we're playing by *Cool Hand Luke* rules, so, yeah, I'm pretty sure.

I then went to my number-one party buddy's apartment in the Avenues, and he put me up in a vacant spare subterranean room below his apartment. It had its own entrance, bathroom, and kitchen, making it easy to get comfortable, and as such, we both saw where this was probably going. After two weeks of reading my nonexistent level of enthusiasm toward finding a rent-paying J.O.B., he called in an exterminator.

Knock knock knock.

"Oh, hi! I was told by the lord upstairs to wait down here!" It's a wild-eyed, flamboyant guy holding a smile that's not necessarily a friendly one. He's already leaning down into the doorway from above, and I step aside, as this technically isn't my place either. I'm feeling strung out, plus the oddness of Chris sending a stranger down here unannounced isn't helping. As he descends the three steps, I observe he's very thin but taut and looks to be Hawaiian. He's wearing a white, high-cut, faux-fox-fur coat over a wifebeater, with extra-high-waisted peach pants that flare out over exposed, sockless ankles, going into caramel-brown mini-platform leather shoes. He has a very slight mustache, and his jet-black hair is slicked all the way back before curving around and below his ears. Giant seventies Oscar de la Renta women's sunglasses further hold it in place. He enters under the low ceiling like a bullfighter from the Andy Warhol Factory as I sit back down in the corner chair. Still smiling that not-so-friendly smile, the size of his pupils makes his eyes black and empty like a shark's, and also like a shark, he doesn't seem to be able to stop moving as he begins doing circles around the confines of the little subterranean dwelling.

"So, this where *you* live?"

"For now ..."

"*Huh*, I should say *so* ..." I can still hear him mutter under his breath with judgy sass, dragging a finger along the dresser top as he moves past it. Still on the move, he inspects his fingertip for dust while holding it up high enough to not break his chin position. I begin to feel a palpable buzzing energy atomizing within his core, which gives him an air of possibly detonating the entire room, but elegantly.

Finally, after three full tours, he stops. "I'm also a photographer, you know. You should let me shoot you sometime." He's looking me up and down now.

"Sure," I answer nonchalantly. Even though I'm still trying to assess this situation, I know I don't like the inflection he'd put on the word *shoot*. I also wonder why he skipped over the first thing he was.

"Listen, the phone isn't working upstairs. Chris said I could make a call down here," he says, speaking as if he's doing a screen test with a put-on authority while reading over lines he's never seen before.

"S-sure," I answer, stuttering once slightly.

He picks up the telephone receiver and sticks it between his cheek and shoulder. "O-o-okay, thna-thnancks a lot!" he stutter-mocks in a nerdy, about-to-sneeze voice, then jumps to deep Elvis—

"H'llo?" Just as fast, he changes to hairdresser's voice. "No, the stand-in is here for some reason. Who should I say is calling? You're kidding!" His tone goes up to very excited. "I, I, I, I don't k-know, I've been up all night reading the report over and over again. Yes, he's right here! Awful." He looks at me while continuing. "Yes, but can you point one of them out in the street?" Looks back down.

"I will I will I will. Oh good, then he doesn't have to go. Oh, he *has* to go. Oh, really? Outrageous."

"Oh, no, no, no, no, no, no, I don't want to frighten anybody unless there's a reason … but listen, we will need to retrain him." He puts his hand over the mouthpiece, looks at me, and whispers, "They are reading the correspondence as we speak it." He looks back at the front door *"Where* is my lab technician? He should be down here by now with the lost marbles." I can hear the rapid *beepbeepbeeping* of a dead line as he hangs up.

Knock knock knock.

We both look at the door, but before I can answer, he says to me in an English butler's voice, "Your elevator has arrived." He then shouts loudly over his shoulder, Brooklyn style, "Who is it?" Turning his head back toward me, he flips his collar up in a 1950s teen drag-race-challenge style and smiles. "*Yess* …?" He faux follows, anxiously waiting. We both are, but for different reasons. The door cracks open just enough to reveal one wide eye.

"Heyy," says my now ex–number one party buddy, to announce the rest of him is going to be coming with.

"Brother, can you spare a di-die-die-dime, I mean line?" He returns by way of wiping the chalkboard clean, yet letting the stutter tip me a wink.

"Heyy, Joel, did you guys meeet? This is Mister Majestic. Mister, this is Joel. What are you guys taalking about?" He's speaking in a laboriously calm way, all syllables drawn out in an overtly fascinated fashion as he slowly moves down the three steps. It's like he's hosting a children's show about deer hunting.

Now we both watch as Mister Majestic begins to do another lap around the room before suddenly stopping in front of where I'm sitting. He extends both of his arms out fully and down toward me, then spreading all his fingertips wide, he touches the tips of his thumbs together. A flurry of miniature white lightning bolts momentarily jiggle all around his fingertips until he jerks his fingers and they fire straight into me. At least that's what his gestures imply.

"*Really?*" I hear myself think out loud.

"C'mon, I'm bored," Mister Majestic quickly announces and without further word, walks up the three steps, leaving the door open behind him.

"Hey man, I'll check you out later?" It's a question that doesn't really feel like a question. He follows out, closing the door behind him.

There was still one trick left up my sleeve, and that

was to just disappear. No explanation to anyone, no witnesses. A vanishing act. *Poof.* Everyone I knew was left to wonder, was I kidnapped? Was I knocked off in a drug deal gone bad? Anton had even wondered as much in a local magazine interview shortly after, but the truth was while they were continuing to play shows now with Mara on percussion (when she wasn't singing "Anemone"), I was doing boring things like detoxing on my parents' couch up in the sticks, while watching things like Oasis on Letterman.

All your dreams are made when you're chained to the mirror and the razor blade ...

How does David Letterman not hear that Liam's singing a commercial for snorting drugs right now? Must be nice to be Oasis. As for me, in some bizarro reality twist after helping to temporarily break them up with the super San Francisco speed snorts on their previous album's tour, now I'm in self-exile while they'd quickly gotten back together and made a classic album that today the whole world is singing the praises of, that is, except maybe George Harrison.

"Wonderwall" was everywhere, and the swagger of the band had grown to such large strides it even seemed to be calling out the Beatles within its lyrics, with their eminent first-ever revisiting of the archives release being the *Anthology* series and the new "comeback" single "Free as a Bird." Whether or not I was reading too much into that, the one thing that was for sure was Britpop had just reached its apex, and I was now officially missing everything. Just a couple of months ago, I was on stage, shaking to "Straight Up and Down," and now I'm standing on my parents' driveway in the middle of nowhere, hoping I can catch a ride with some random space aliens that might happen to be flying overhead.

I gaze along the row of houses across the street, which are much larger than the ones on my parents' side. The street is functioning as a physical border to indicate the neighborhood's financial differences. Those houses over on that side of the street are still pretty much exactly the same in style, but with a second story more of whatever it is. Like a fast-food double cheeseburger.

A few houses down on the other side is Chad, the only neighbor around here I'd come to know. Chad is sitting in the driveway on a lawn chair with knees as spread apart as they will go. His short-sleeve yellow tropical Aloha print shirt is unbuttoned all the way and spread wide. Other than his longish blond locks, the only other visible body hair is on his legs, which look overly skinny due to the extra-wide board shorts he's wearing. Naturally, flip-flops complete the look. There's another empty folded-out chair next to him that maybe his imaginary surfer bro is sitting in, or it's just in case a stray nomad female impossibly happens to walk by in this middle-center of the barren rural-slash-suburban graveyard.

"Aloha! You got any rolling papers?" he shouts.

"Nah, man. Not these days. What's goin' on?"

"*Comme ci, comme ça*, my monsieur," he returns almost in the right context. "Hey, nice tracksuit!"

He's referring to the indigo with white striped Adidas suit I'm wearing. The one good thing Oasis's goofy sports style did for me was to provide some Britpop identity connection while dressing undercover.

"Feel free to come over and chalk a brah, dude! Your scales must be dry!"

"Suure." I walk over and take the empty seat as he reaches in the Igloo cooler just behind him. He's got white pasty cream on his nose, though we're a million miles from any beach. Then, he unfolds a metal suntanning reflector and peers into it. "I think my crow's feet are getting worse. It's the eyes that go first, dude, remember that. Been using my mom's Oil of Olay, but I don't think it's working." He tilts his head back and angles the reflector.

Chad is ex-party person royalty turned fallen loser who, for untold reasons, had been reduced to moving back in with his mother. Here we were, two party fuck-ups from different worlds, now living back with our parents, sitting in a driveway and drinking beer together in exile. The thing I had on him was he was older and pushing thirty, and also unlike me, a relic of a lost period he couldn't grow up from or return to. Like a French plantation in Vietnam, he was frozen in a place and time that had moved on. Those were his best days, and he was holding on to them for as long as his mother would let him. This all reinforced to me that today was the day I was going to rip apart my address book until I'd sleuthed out a room to rent back in San Francisco. It would be smarter to wait until I had a little more money, but trying to be smart was officially starting to bug me.

If I didn't get some nightlife, some night *club* life soon, I was gonna break orbit in the bad way, as in into my inner depths of black, broken-record orbit. I longed for the night people and the views from both on and off the stages with booze-stocked bars, the dressed-to-live-it people, the *life*. San Francisco–sized life, one of the world's great post-nightlife walking cities. In that morning twilight, when for that first hour while starting toward home you and only a few other stray nameless *own* it. The gray twinkling coolness to the concrete sidewalks and enormous architecture, the electric-green cypress tree–filled parks that glow, pregnant with dew and ancient new awakenings. Heightened color that makes me *feel* everything.

"Hey, wanna watch *The Mask*? Just came to HBO man. My mom gets a hundred and fifty channels, a hundred and *fif*-ty, bro. Wicked selects. How about another Corona?"

"Nah."

Some months later, I took my fourteen-year-old sister to her first big concert, which was taking place at the San Jose State Event Center for the KOME radio station's festival "Almost Acoustic Christmas." Nineties garbage like Garbage, No Doubt, Toadies, The Rentals, Everclear, and Tripping Daisy all succeed in making me join my sister in being excited to see Radiohead and Sonic Youth, but I'm really only here for Oasis.

They hit the stage with their "Morning Glory" guns a-blazing, and it makes me feel a million miles away from being who I was, now sitting up here watching them from the stands instead of sharing the stage. I knew that I'd soon go much crazier than I would spinning out on mass class-A drugs, and knowing in my soul that BJM were also on the way to next-level success. It was now more than ever that I had to get back. "Supersonic," "Hello," "Roll with It," and "Live Forever" all have lyrics that rubbed my current situation raw, and then Liam leaves the stage so Noel can sing a solo "Wonderwall" and "Don't Look Back in Anger," both of which somehow manage to take my sad predicament up a whole other level.

Then Liam is back strutting with arms swinging in his oversized fuzzy mint-colored sweater and perfect Beatles *Revolver* hair as "Champagne Supernova" begins, and the song couldn't hit home any harder. Little did I know that on this same night and at this exact same moment in time, December 16, Mara and BJM were back in SF playing at Starcleaners.

Where were you while we were getting high?

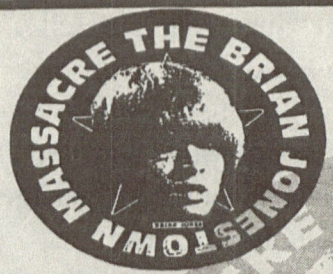

The Brian Jonestown Massacre are truly out of their heads. Here we are in San Francisco, a.k.a. Hippie Heaven, but these guys are saying it with dead flowers and Beatle boots. If 60's were 90's, then the so-called Beautiful People have been sent to oblivion, all postage paid with an Altamont commemerative stamp. The Brian Jonestown Massacre have crashed the party, and you best believe the Kool-Aid has been dosed! The band has been standing in the shadows of night for a couple of years now, wowing the faithful with their motorpsychedelic sound. They seemed to be playing unrelentlessly, but not catching the hood-winked eye of the masses. All that seems to be changing right now. To bake a mind altering cake these days, you've got to smash a few sugarcubes. The band happens to fit in nicely with the latest wave of British pop (poppie?) groups that are influenced by the swirling sounds of a fine farfisa organ.

After watching Rolling Stones videos and discussing Small Faces lyrics, I was impressed by the fact that they seemed to be more than pretty things with groovy haircuts. It's scary, but with the BJTM, it's not just a band, it's an adventure. A way of life. They walk it like they talk it, with the prerequisite rock star attitude.

Founder and visionary Anton is joined by the legendary Matt Hollywood on bass, while Brian Not Jones is behind the drum kit, holding everything together with a solid backbeat. When guitarist Jeff Davies plugs in, he layers an icing of sweet soul over the cake. Newest member Joel is a gas to watch onstage. He 's the self appointed hip shaker /scene maker type, shaking the maracas and the tamborine with equal vigor. Anton has the mesmerizing vocalist bit down. When he isn't strangling his guitar to death, he's strutting his stuff topless in true Iggy style, right down to the microphone shoved down his unbuttoned pants. That's groovy, but I say finish what you start! Why be such a tease - once your pants are undone already, you should be obligated to offer comparisons with the microphone, or else keep that thing undercover to begin with! Anyway...

When BJTM play live the explosive energy comes together and blows your speedometer to 110. At the recent show they opened for hot British pop tarts, Oasis, the band managed to turn two songs into an entire set. Band tensions were mounting, with guitars untuned and unplayed - the crowd were mesmerized seemingly see the band disintegrate before their very eyes - the energy level at it's peak. All the rage came out in a frenzied chaos onstage in front of the unsuspecting crowd. Far from being a disaster, this turned out to be one of the band's best shows ever! Expect the unexpected when you go and see them play, who can tell if they'll even bother to show up themselves! Just kidding- you're sure to experience true satisfaction with this band!

Should the Brian Jones Town Massacre manage to hold it together it seems they are destined for great things. They were recently nominated for a WAMMIE in the "Far Out And Beyond" category, though they were pipped at the post by Billy Nayer. It is about the only pigeon hole it is seems safe to put them in. Anything less just wouldn't be worth shaking your maracas at!

MICHELLE C. ASTRO

Things are starting to happen for BJM in the Bay Area music scene rags

The Brian Jonestown Massacre

Band returns from South By Southwest with only slight injuries

by Amanda-Jane

Everything should be brilliant next year, if we don't kill each other."

So said Anton Newcombe, guitarist/vocalist/crystal ball-gazer for The Brian Jones Town Massacre in the fall of 1995.

Flash to March 1996 and we are in Austin, Texas, for the massive Record Industry schmooze-fest that is South By South West, in the super-plush lobby of the Four Seasons hotel. About 400 record executives are drinking up their expense accounts, speaking incredibly loud so we all know they are working unbelievably hard. Across the lobby I spy three figures that have more rock n' roll in their thrift store outfits than the rest

If you can get away from the histrionics and temper tantrums, they are probably one of the most consistently good bands that San Francisco has to offer.

of the room together. It's none other than Dean (guitarist), Brian (drums) and Joel (maracas, shades and looking cool) from the Brian Jonestown Massacre. Within a few minutes, they have regaled me with the sordid details of the previous night's gig. Everything was going just swell until Matt Hollywood (bass) and Anton fell out. Really fell out. The resulting punch up left Anton with a broken wrist, fleeing back to SF and Matt spending the rest of the trip holed up in true recluse fashion in their motel room.

Are they worried? Are they distressed? Well, only about the fact they can't locate any free booze, but they've weathered storms before. Brian simply shrugs, "If we just stayed in the studio and put stuff out, we shouldn't tour..." After all, we are talking about the band that grabbed the much coveted opening slot with the best eyebrows in Brit-Pop, Oasis, when they played at the Bottom of the Hill. What happened? They

finally took to the stage whilst guitarist Jeff was still out scoring dope. That saw the end of his collaboration with the Brian Jones Town. Then Joel went missing for a few months, supposedly "rescued" from the debauchery of the music biz by his parents. He is back now and unrepentant as ever. People have come and gone, but to this point Anton and Matt have always held it together. What happens next is anyone's guess, but not one of the band even mentioned folding.

If you can get away from the histrionics and temper tantrums, they are probably one of the most consistently good bands that San Francisco has to offer. Their live shows are an experience and they go all out to make it so. "We really just experiment with where we could take the sound. We had a song we'd close with that would last between six and 12 minutes, people would go, 'yeah that's the make out song,' and at every show we would have the drunk hippy spinning around." They have built the buzz around their live shows themselves. Until recently, they've been pretty much ignored by the press, but that has been changing since Fall saw the release of their first full length CD album, *Methadrone*. A collection of their greatest moments over the past few years, it brings together songs put out on cassettes and singles, and is eminently listenable. Doused with a British Jesus and Mary Chain era flavor, it could claim the Velvet Underground as its main influence. Spacey, sparse guitar layers, mumbling, intoxicated lyrics, the painfulness of being. Anton works like a man possessed (and there are many who would say he is), words tumbling out of him as he tries to explain what he can hear in his head. He talks of the "simpleness" of music, but the Brian Jonestown Massacre deliver an intricate mess of sound. "Sixties style, but not retro," declares Anton. ◪

also watershed   mod

the brian jonestown massacre

can you stand it.

tangible records in association with the united kingdom prese

monday sept. 26th

oasis

@the bottom of the hill
1233 17th st. at texas

BJM's flyer for our opening slot with Oasis three nights
before they—well, you know…

SONIC BOOM: Dark Hippies and Wicked Poppers
THE BRIAN JONESTOWN MASSACRE INTERVIEW

member, although recently he's been kidnapped by his parents and is now in Sanora somewhere.

He got snatched away by his parents?
Yeah well, that isn't forever. We have a lot of resources, more than somebody's family, so we'll get him back for sure. I mean what are you going to do? Live on a farm, or are you going to go tour the world? I'm sure his family loves him and all that, but the show must go on.

Is it safe to say that you and Matt Hollywood are the core of the group, since you two do most of the song writing?
No, I consider the core being the whole group, since we all go through so much with practicing and stuff.

You're in the studio now recording, and I guess you have the guys from PSYCHIC TV on hand producing, is that correct?

Just two weeks later in my new little black room at the drug warehouse in San Francisco on the morning of New Year's Day, 1996

Record Stories

Lush camphor trees sway next to palms in the sunny
California easy breeze of the United States's 1976
bicentennial year of independence. Outdoor suburban
shopping centers sprawl in every direction, mostly
designed as if the Knights of the Round Table relocated
the gadzooks biz to Guadalajara. My mom pulls her
slightly used Corvette money red Chevette into the Tower
Records parking lot on Bascom Avenue in Campbell, the
neighboring part of San Jose where my parents and older
brother Paul live in Cambrian Park. I survey the drive-thru
restaurant-sized yellow with red *TOWER RECORDS* sign
perched on a sunbaked faded yellow brick stand that
matches the store's arched villa-like large windows. This
is a new shopping parking lot for me, and by the size of
this place, it looks like the music selection is going to be
far beyond the small record section in the Gemco
department store where my mother had bought me The
Beatles's *Red* and *Blue* double-album compilations. It was
obvious even to me, as a current six-year-old, that this was
a much more serious record store experience, and life in
my brother's eight-year-old age group was getting more
real out there, and the social pressures were rising beyond
the cut of your Schwinn Stingray motocross bicycle.

Riffing guitar rock was the brand-new rebel sensation
for the college and teen scenes, with the ginormous

behemoth that is the record business already reaching well into pre-teen and now even deeper down into my brother's age group. Surfing, skateboarding, kustom van culture, Frisbees, hairy chests, knee-high socks, and terry cloth headbands—this all seemingly went better with heavy riffs and wailing solos.

What I'm saying is we are in the ultimate California 1970s suburbs. Land of the lefties, but then, six-year-olds don't know anything about that or why some people think any one person would be treated differently from another. Every kid my age had been learning to live on *Sesame Street* their whole lives so far, which was a public television children's program with a fully integrated cast and filmed on a set motifed after a New York Harlem-type neighborhood street which, during its first season in 1969, had become a cultural phenomenon. I was born two weeks into season two of the show which, and in true "TV baby" fashion, my mother started putting my crib in front of our TV as an afternoon distraction before I could even hold a spoon, to a place where all types and colors lived together as equals, taken even further to include friendly, people-like, hairy Muppet monsters that came in all the colors of the crayon rainbow.

Despite the one- to five-year-old target age group, the show was experimental for the time in a smart and often oddball hippie way that it also won over the stoned college crowd. This was largely due to the animated segments like the funky sounds of the "Pinball Number Count," sung by an unknown-at-the-time Pointer Sisters, backed by jazz musicians and recorded in San Francisco's Tenderloin District. It was a very early lesson in both groovin' and counting while shooting around a psychedelic "Yellow Submarine"-style animated pinball game world. Then there was Grace Slick of Jefferson Airplane counting to ten in the bizarrely urgent "Jazz Spies," and of course sixties Italio-soundtrack maestro Piero Umiliani's "Mah Nà Mah Nà" Euro-lounge jingle.

There were also live musical guests like Stevie Wonder performing "Superstition," Nina Simone rendering at the height of her early-seventies powers, conga king Ray Barretto, Ray Charles singing the alphabet, Jose Feliciano, Judy Collins, Lou Rawls, Johnny Cash, Malvina Reynolds, Paul Simon, and on and on. This was all so instrumental to the soulful importance of music set within me, infusing the life path while being an audience of one perched in my high chair, flinging green peas.

Even in the outside-the-house world, music was always a constant, whether out with my mother grocery shopping or hitting the many department stores, the car radio was always turned to the contemporary soul station, and when my dad was in a rare moment of being sick of the Doobie Brothers, on trips to the library in his van, we'd listen to the sounds of the local college soul-jazz funk-fusion radio show.

Now with my recent sixth birthday, I had officially moved past the show's targeted age group and was now, unbeknownst to me, symbolically making my transition by walking into my first record store. My excited brother pushes through the doors first, releasing a blast of Thin Lizzy's "Jailbreak" into my face as my mother catches the door, and he is gone into the crowded fray. For me it's like walking inside of a giant television, or else this is like the K-Tel Records television commercials but outside of the TV as some new real world. *K-Tel presents Blockbuster! A great new LP! Twenty original hits! Original stars! KC & The Sunshine Band! Alice Cooper! Average White Band! War! Heart! Edgar Winter Group and many more! Elton John! The Hollies! The Osmonds! The Commodores! Miracles! The Bay City Rollers! Blockbuster! Twenty original hits! Original stars! Be sure to get the best from K-Tel! LP $5.99, tape $6.99!*

My mother is confused as to how to begin navigating all this overwhelming commotion because it's been a while since her teenybopper Beatles years. We just pick the nearest aisle and start walking along the packed racks of vinyl that seem to go on in a maze for miles, stuffed in tiered rows exploding with album artwork. In fact, the whole interior is like an explosion of images and excited lettering on signs, posters plastering the walls, and cardboard sale signs; genre sections hang everywhere by strings from the roof. Electric guitar rock is at its maximum bloated height, with the Ramones having only just released the first punk rock album, but all genres that currently make money are represented. Posters advertising new albums like Stevie Wonder's *Songs in the Key of Life* promo poster hang next to Bob Seger beardly advertising *Night Moves*, next to Peter Tosh *Legalize It*, next to "vintage" late-sixties pictures of Mick Jagger, the Beatles, and on and on everywhere.

It's almost like a training ground for the rock club experience with the brick-heavy arched window-wall scheme keeping the natural light low. The narrow aisles are hard for us to navigate because it's so crowded with overly excited or completely detached people, and I go wide-eyed at the colorful, almost entirely pre-legal adult crowd. There are more bells in here than all the churches in Dublin, and it's as if they are the only way pants come, six-year-old me's included.

I've been starting to notice lately that girls are kinda neat. There's as many of them in here as boys, and they sure do dress nicer than the girls in my first-grade class. Big sunglasses, every kind of shoe in platform height, turtlenecks, short-shorts, wide-leg pants, high-slit skirts, knee-high zip boots, huge hoopy earrings, patchwork denim, head scarves, lower-than-low-rise jeans, stripey stockings and sweaters, casual jumpsuits, tight vests, block-heeled sandals, crocheted sweaters, metallic tights, ruffly crop-tops, choker necklaces, halter tops, barely buttoned-up button-downs, and more things that I don't even know the names of yet.

White teen wispy mustaches with feathered hair abound in flocks of different colored tank tops, and the people behind the counter look like they have an air of royalty about them. The one who seems like he would be king is all feathers and blond fluffy perfection down to his shoulders.

A lot of the record covers look kind of creepy, the intentional attempts at looking "dangerous" in a new more hardline version of separating the kids from the adults. AC/DC, Judas Priest, Alice Cooper—hard rockers are a very menacing bunch, seemingly. I'm only six, so it's working. I find the letter A and from there can quickly find my way to the Beatles section. There are many, many

Beatles albums here, and every single record in the whole place has varying numbers in front of $ _.99 price tags on it. I start internally counting in Pointer Sisters style, but this all quickly goes beyond my educational television math skills. The one thing I do know is you'd have to be a *millionaire* to have all the music in here!

My brother suddenly appears out of the crowd, excitedly clutching the new KISS *Rock and Roll Over* album, which will insure his up-to-date status with his tribe of other striped terry-cloth-head and wristband-wearing danger-seeking eight-year-olds. My mom has even gotten swept up in the barely under-the-radar frenzy everyone is in and buys the before-mentioned new Stevie Wonder album. Later that day, dressed in just a pair of blue Adidas track shorts and gigantic black leather headphones, my surrounding outer world is awash in greens, oranges, golds, and browns, representing the current early 1970s decor trends. The one and only concern in my whole world at this moment is maintaining the perfect balance of dancing with semi-abandon while still having enough reserve to keep the giant adult-sized earphones from falling off my head. These leather-lined headphones are heavy and cupping the entire sides of my head as *Isn't she lovely* ... surrounds in the key of life. As I internally replay all of the new sensations from my first record store experience today, I can feel its pull taking me all the way.

I'd also just become old enough to start playing school sports, and so my mother enrolled me in the San Jose, California Cambrian Pal Soccer League. My team, the Jaguars, were in just a few short games revealed to be the worst team in the entire local soccer league. Although I was given the goalie position, the one semi-stationary role in the whole game, I was worked out the hardest, as every Saturday game day, the latest opposing team would spend the entire duration totally bombarding me with the ball.

Although this was an important moment in first showing me how to be a "team player," one of a group trying to make the same thing happen together, whenever my team actually did get control of the ball, which was usually by a mistake of the opposing team, something bad would happen. Things like my own teammates unexpectedly kicking the ball past me into our own goal by accident or kicking each other in the shin and sending one another to the ground crying. They were my friends, but it was frustrating being unchallenged as the real-life *Bad News Bears* of San Jose soccer, a recent hit movie that had just run on television for the first time. Although I'd loved it, I didn't want to relate to it as much as I did.

Every game ended with each team exchanging a "good game" type of chant to each other in unison. "Two, four, six, eight, who do we appreciate …" followed by shouting one another's team names in a "hip-hip-hooray" fashion. The always-victorious opposing team never failed to shout it out loud and enthusiastically, often with a few giggles along the way as we, the regular losers, would speed-mumble through, then hurriedly get off the field.

One Saturday during a particularly heavy beating, I was left in a rare moment of peace, while my other teammates actually, for once, got the ball across the field and near the opposing team's goal. Using my hand as a sun visor, I squinted to make out the faraway action. Then, I moved my surveying gaze over to the full but bored crowd of parents and schoolkids sitting in the aluminum bleachers. As usual, the unscored ball was kicked back in my direction from all the way across the field until bouncing its way down to a slow roll and stopping a few feet in front of me. With all the other players now so far away, I had all the time I wanted to set up the biggest return I could muster. All the attention of both the full bleachers and both teams across the field were now focused and waiting on me and my return kick.

I go into such an overcompensating wind-up kick that despite nailing the ball hard, I flipped myself into the air awkwardly and landed flat out on the grass. I remained there motionless with my head half buried sideways in the untrimmed green while watching the well-kicked ball rise high, higher, up up high and away until it reached the lofty top of its trajectory when suddenly, worrisomely, it took a hanger curve and started falling toward the sidelines. It was now coming down hard and fast and right toward a young soccer mom sitting on the field near the grassy sideline. She was holding a compact mirror and fixing her makeup, totally unawares.

The crash-slamming meteorlike ball landed right on her huge brown leather sack purse, completely exploding all of its contents. The wind generated from the blast blew her long, feathered hair back as her denim bell-bottoms whooshed like an open-end underwater sea creature attempting a quick escape.

Her purse didn't just explode. I mean, this huge brown purse was like the Big Bang, shooting out what seemed like an entire universe of items in every direction, made of hair products, bobby pins, a brush, perfume, floss, Tic Tacs, hand lotion, ChapStick, notepad, nailfile, checkbook, prescription bottles, cigarettes, change purse, nail clippers, tissues, Bic lighter, address book, Chiclets gum, aspirin, pens, loose receipts, a box of Raisinets, sunglasses, cough drops, tampons, mail, a paperback book, flare gun, and a huge double key ring, both of which were filled with keys that jingle-jangle-drone vibrate off of each other in multi-mid-air tingle-tones until all at once they hit the ground in unison, chiming like a giant tambourine beat.

She shrieked in shocked surprise, and her makeup compact flew from her hand as she quickly covered her face with both hands. This was some other kid's mother, and I was going to be in big trouble. I continued to remain motionless, flat on the ground and even attempted to push my body further down, in hopes of disappearing into the unkempt grass. Then, in the silent moment, she slowly spread apart two fingers covering one of her eyes. Her hands then slowly came down. All eyes were on her now. As I prepared myself for the worst, rather than revealing red-faced anger, she instead threw her head back and laughed hysterically at the sight of all the purse contents surrounding her in every direction. The crowd of silent, frozen-in-the-moment parents behind her in the stands, seeing this tension-releasing reaction, now all joined in on the laughter. I slowly lifted my head up from the grass as the cheering and the laughter spread and got louder. That's when the light bulb went up. If you're gonna blow it, blow it so big that it must be celebrated as a victory.

TAKE ACID NOW

and come see

with Hollowbody
and Nebtwister

Live Music until 2 AM

@ the PEACOCK LOUNGE
552 HAIGHT st.

Next to the Horseshoe

Believe It

Encroach Hotel

I wake up on the sticky carpet of a motel room floor and straight into a spaghetti Western–style extreme close-up stare-down standoff with a medium-sized cockroach. The drama levels of this instant showdown are in tune with Donovan's "Season of the Witch," the soundtrack provided from Anton's small boombox sitting on the beat-up nightstand next to the beat-down queen-sized bed. I'm not at all happy with this brand of "good morning" into the day, the cockroach in my face I mean. I guess I could be thankful it's not a *giant* roach, but still just as totally gross and one that most surely belongs to the crew we saw crawling on the white walls until lights out, when they would have commenced making their many pass-overs of my body here on the floor. The motel door is open, and it is, of course, already hot and blindingly sunny in Los Angeles today, despite the faint presence of a slight breeze up here on the second floor.

Anton suddenly appears in the doorway, with one hand holding a telephone receiver up to his ear and the other dangling the plastic base from two fingers, "… and so what was in my mind was …" and then he is gone, his voice trailing away as long as the motel room telephone cord will allow, and he's back, framed in the doorway again in dark silhouette with the blasting LA sun behind him. "… so we do this thing live where …" and he's out of view again, keeping in constant movement as he does a magazine interview.

I ping the bug across the room, knowing it's only a temporary solution, as it is Anton, Sophie, and I who are the temporary guests in this roach's motel, just outside of the hip Silverlake neighborhood.

"… but then they killed all of it …"

The sound of the muffled rickety bathroom fan stops, and now Sophie opens the door and prowls catlike over to the disheveled queen-sized bed, then curls up against the headboard. Her hair is sprayed up in a rat's nest, kind of like mine, but less Beatles with bangs, with hers frozen up into the spray fray. Her black sleeveless turtleneck is a nice compromise with looking great and accepting today's tempts. Tight white jeans lead down to tall, black, leather lace-up mod boots to round out the look.

"… and all this other crap …"

Anton is also in white jeans, a flowy white shirt from the India Imports store we went to at our Berkeley stop-off yesterday, signifying his reign of fashion sensibility when it comes to dressing in hot-ass LA.

"That's nothing. It's like when people …"

I, on the other hand, am in all black, with the red ringer trims of my T-shirt being the only other color on me. He stops in the doorway this time and surveys the recent changes in movement. "Well, it is, and it isn't …" Then he's gone again.

I have every reason to believe we're down here on a scoping trip of sorts for possible new moves, but still, I don't want to jinx it by asking.

"… it's unimaginable now that it's 1997, but here's

the thing ..."

Like, if I put it out there in sonic form, then that's reason enough to cancel the thought. The three of us have been isolated up in Portland for so long now, and the band's wheels have for the first time been in a prolonged state of motionlessness.

"I just try my best ..."

There are demos recorded from up there to get things going somewhere else for real now, and I hold on tight to my silent wishes as I take my turn to wash up in the bathroom. A few minutes later, I'm out.

"... or, whatever the fuck ..."

Our self-isolation up in the Northwest—which for me was a lifesaving detour after my return to San Francisco and life in a LSD-manufacturing warehouse that almost led me to thirty-to-life—had also coincided with the world's exciting mid-nineties musical times having started to turn into something else for the late nineties. Especially down here, the music world of today felt like we'd somehow reentered into an alternate-universe version of where we'd only just left it. Our nineties-style sixties-mindedness seemed have to disappeared again, but yet here we were, out on the fabled Highway 61, thought to have disappeared from the maps many years ago. Not that that was necessarily always a positive road to be riding on in the first place.

"... I don't give a good *goddamn* ..."

I felt like we were outlaws on the run, holed up in this motel, Butch, Sundance and Etta Place, Bonnie, Clyde and W. D. Jones, undercover music outlaws in a world that if it knew their intent and purpose, then there would be trouble. Having said all that, I can't totally rule out the fact that maybe this is all just inside my head.

"… I mean, fuck that shit … look at what happened …"

Beyond the Donovan two-disc collection *Troubadour* and Dylan's *Highway 61*, Anton's boombox will only play our new Brian Jonestown Massacre demos, and that is all, which I'm fine with. It's these three sounds that make up our bubble's soundtrack during this time zone of the life trip. Outside, nothing else matters.

"… then go for it … you just have to go out there and get it. That's all I have to say on that."

Anton walks into the room. "Hey, you guys ready?" The phone blings a muffled *briingg* with its flop onto the nightstand. That means "ouch" in telephone talk, which ironically doesn't have many words in its own language. "Let's get out of this dump."

Ten minutes later, we're checked out of the Roach Motel and are pulling underneath the metal canopy roof of a nearby Mobil station. Sophie's in the passenger's seat, pulling out her sketchbook, while I hang outside my open door with minor bebop inflections upon the roof, then settle in stance as if just waiting for the police pat-down. Anton pumps gas into the tank while periodically looking side to side. We were always looking.

It's just getting hotter, and so the leather jacket comes back off as I trade views of the graffitied Phil's Transport & Storage concrete building on one corner of the wide intersection and the even more graffitied Atlas Van Lines building on the opposite. Atlas wins my graffiti competition, thanks to its more traditional old school hip-hop stylings, while Phil's is just kind of a goofy monster. Then I absentmindedly try to peer my way through to the snack shop's back wall cooler doors just to see if this one carries beer, even though it is not going to affect me any in the state my pants pockets are in, but still, just because I don't know. Looks like they don't carry beer at this one, or anything else I care for anyway. I'm so sick of shitty chips and the like, thanks to the everyday broke trips to the Plaid Pantry convenience store around the corner from the shitty punk rock band factory practice space we were illegally living in back up in Portland. Anyway, now I can shoot the idea down ceremoniously in my hea—

Click. The gas tank is full.

Turns out we were on our way to what would become our new Bottom of the Hill of sorts, in the "home turf venue" sense, Spaceland. Anton wants to talk to their promoter about playing a show there, because sometimes just showing up is better than calling someone. These are the only two forms of communication available, unless you want to send a stamped letter in the mail to get a conversation going, which isn't very practical.

Spaceland is sort of retro–German Tudor in style, with a shingled roof and white faux half-timbered frontal design. We walk inside its dark interior, and Anton immediately heads toward the bar to ask for the club's promoter. There is music playing loudly, but as it is not at all my thing, I don't hear it. I mean, I can *hear* it, physically, but it's more like audio interference, like static. Nobody *listens* to static, I mean pay attention to the changes or whatever. It's just there for some reason. A guy then comes out of the back and does a lot of head nodding while Anton talks closely in his ear. LA better get ready.

As we pull away, switching back and forth from my double-back-window views, I ponder actually living down here. This is where, only a few months ago, it had all gone down for us. I mean the directional kind of down. They should have called it "The Johnny Depp's Viper Room Massacre," but the one thing that we thought was for sure at the time was neither San Francisco nor Portland was going to get us anywhere, next level speaking.

We get back in the car and drive to Bomp! Records owner Greg Shaw's house, who by this point has released *Methodrone*, *Take It from the Man!*, *Their Satanic Majesties' Second Request*, *Thank God for Mental Illness*, and most of the early BJM seven-inch singles. Everything there is yeah, sure, great, and whatever until suddenly Greg, Anton, and Sophie are going out to "run errands," as Greg puts it, and just like that, I'm going to be babysitting his five-year-old son, Tristan.

Tristan is in his usual mini version of his dad's daily uniform of baggy 501's and a loud tie-dye T-shirt in the familiar rainbow color combination. They leave us sitting on the living room couch together.

"So, uh ... you wanna watch TV or something?" I ask, hoping I can immediately disengage from this unexpected situation.

"No," Tristan replies without missing a beat.

"Play outside?"

"No."

"Play with your toys?"

"No," he says again, officially turning the conversation into a duo call-and-response-style song of

70

mutual disinterest. "I wanna play Monopoly."

"Monopoly?" I ask, somewhat in disbelief. I fucking hate Monopoly. A game that teaches kids how to be greedy landlords. Plus, that shit is boring as fuck, I'd like to say in all honesty to him, but that's not the kind of language we use here, as I remember it, a remembrance that I'm pretty sure signifies that I'm suddenly becoming a pretty great babysitter. "What else besides that can we do?"

"Nothing."

"Wanna watch TV?"

"No." Why a sixties garage rock guru's kid wants to play a game like that boggles my perspectives on the matter, but then suddenly it mutually doesn't matter.

"*I* think that you should leave. *Now* "

What's up with this brat? "Well, your dad told me to babysit you."

He gets up off the couch and walks to the middle of the room. "Get! Out! Of! My! *House!*"

That last bit came with a James Brown drop to knees for dramatic effect, and this is all a bit much for me right now, this son of satanic majesties' second request, and so I get up and go to the refrigerator. It's weirdly kind of full but yet with nothing to eat, all half-empty condiment containers and nothing readily edible until finally, after more sleuthing, I find some deli counter salami hiding in the back for some reason. I open it up and put a slice in my mouth, but the salami explodes on my tongue like its been dipped in chemical acid. I quickly snatch it from inside my face, then read the expiration date, which was three months ago.

Meanwhile, Tristan's disappeared, hopefully to go play in the middle of Silverlake Boulevard or something, and so I go back to the couch and start eyeing Greg's giant wall of CDs. I'm preparing my deep sixties dive when a few minutes later, Tristan nonchalantly comes out of his bedroom holding a large yellow-and-blue space rifle. He looks guilty in that way kids do when they are bluffing about being a nice guy. Now wanting to be my friend again, seemingly, he jumps up on the couch next to me, his head tilted to the side like guilty in-progress little kids do as his long over-bowled locks flop up and down like they're a crowd doing the wave at a game. Then he sets down his big rocket blaster, reaches right out, and gently pulls on a stalk of my Aqua Net rat's nest.

"Your hair feels like it died," he says, twisting the longish plastered hair branch between two fingers.

I don't care for this diagnosis too much, but he's suddenly funny in that too naturally psychedelically synced-up-for-his-own-good way. It's strangely a bonding moment and probably saved me from death by plastic rocket gun bullet. I have to wonder which internal side of his will win—his natural psychedelic child's intuitiveness or the Man's brainwashing board games and space rocket guns.

Some bottom-shelf sleuthing of the vast CD shelves reveals some music video cassettes, like The Small Faces video collection, bootlegs like Bob Dylan's *Eat The Document*, David Bowie's *Cracked Actor*, The Rolling Stones' *Rock and Roll Circus*, and The Monkees' *Head*, which were rare finds.

As soon as I pull one out, they are back, and as the

door opens, I ask, "Wow, man, Greg, you have so many cool videos—is it okay to watch some of these?"

"No, no. I'm sorry, it's not possible for you to watch anything because something with all the TV wires and connections needs to be fixed, and I just haven't had the time to figure it out yet."

Apparently, Greg has offered to let us sleep here tonight, and later, when he retires to his psychedelic chambers for the evening, I can't stop thinking how cool it would be to watch some of these videos. Eventually, everyone else dozes off and I attempt to fix his connection setup so I can watch the videos. After unplugging and switching around a lot more than I wind up plugging back in, I somehow get the picture and sound going on the TV screen. I'd find out on our next trip down here that I'd just completely screwed everything else up so much worse that he would have to call in a home electronics expert to sort it all out.

First, I throw on the bootleg of *Rock and Roll Circus*. The long-overdue official release coming later in the year will lose almost all of the otherworldly dimensional chaos provided from this multigenerational, redubbed boot, with all its picture loss and extra-thick grainy black-and-white insanity-portal-into-hell vision version I was watching now. I watch the Stones perform "Sympathy for the Devil" over and over again, each time with my nose closer and closer to the screen. Mick is in demonic androgyny shaman mode, while Brian Jones provides me with my lifelong "That Girl Suicide" maraca-shaking pattern.

Afterward, I watch vintage Small Faces television performances, then The Monkees' feature film *Head*, before going back to the Stones clip again and again. The sun begins to rise. Oh yeah, I forgot to mention along with the white Indian shirt Anton acquired in the bay on our way down, I'd acquired something else white colored that had gone to my head throughout the night.

Two hours later, the living room phone rings. A well-slept Sophie picks it up expecting a call, but it's for me.

"Jooel, this is *Ondi*." Ondi is one of the *Dig!* documentary filmmaker siblings.

"Ondi!"

"Soo lovely to hear your voice, *darling*. Listen, it just so happens my brother David and I are doing camera work on a video shoot for The Monkees. We're sitting here right now, talking about how incredible it would be to somehow sneak you on camera with them for the documentary."

"*What?* Come and get me."

I hang up the phone. Having just watched the Monkees in *Head* only a few hours ago, this level of coincidence rightly has me tripping at next levels. Because the Monkees had a TV show in regular daily afternoon syndication, as a toddler still barely able to even walk, I'd watch them high up from my highchair perch, having my 3 p.m. snack while transfixed on Mother's other little helper, the television.

Because they didn't play their own instruments for the first two records, they'd been labeled a "fake" band, but when I got old enough to know what's up on my own, I discovered that they were actually just as legit as many of the "authentic" bands in the LA scene at the time. Not only Monkees records, but others like the Byrds breakout first single—*cough*—"Mr. Tambourine Man," the Beach

Boys album *Pet Sounds*, and a lot more than people realize were mostly recorded by the session musicians, "the Wrecking Crew." Take that session collective out of the chemical equation, and a massive chunk of what made the sixties "the sixties" vanishes from the blotter paper.

After playing their own instruments on successive Monkees records, they couldn't ditch the stigma, and so, in a premeditated self-sabotage, they made the image-destroying film that was *Head*, which despite now being considered one of the most important works of rock-and-roll cinema, also managed to be career destroying for all band members except Mike Nesmith, who went on to legitimacy by helping to innovate the "country rock" sound, a style he'd already been representing with his own songs on the original show. Scriptwriter Jack Nicholson would go on to be actor Jack Nicholson, and the creators of the Monkees, Bob Rafelson and Bert Schneider, would next go on to produce a little thing called *Easy Rider*.

David picks me up in their dusty SUV about twenty minutes later. I really like David; he has a combination of no-nonsense and a gentle way that's easy to be around in all the uneasy ways that he'd be traveling with us in the coming weeks to months to years. It is, of course, already hotter than blazes out here in the real world's get-up-and-go morning time. I hate it but I don't let it get me down, as David has offered to pick me up a half-pint of vodka on the way. Then I'd have insurance that no matter which way this thing went, I'd feel good going there. I also knew he was more than happy to help supply me with some *"Joel will do something crazy on camera* juice."

We pull up to the studio. "Okay, when we go in, act

like nothing is going on. I'm going to get back to work while you just hang to the side and think of a way for us to get you in this somehow."

"Right on," I return, implying some sort of confidence in what I'm doing that I do not actually have. We enter the building, and David gets us past reception, then quickens his pace, leaving me behind to start my secret mission. Just beyond the entryway is a hallway of doors leading to the soundstage. I slowly sway into a stroll as suddenly the first door flies open to reveal a hurried Mike Nesmith. He's decked out in a white-on-white suit ensemble, looking like an old-man version of himself from the "Circle Sky" scene in *Head*. Here the flamboyant Carnaby Street collar ruffles have been replaced with tissues inserted to keep the heavy pancake makeup job from rubbing off onto his collar. He looks to me as if "oh no," but I slide to the side, letting him pass unfettered. He was always my favorite.

I cautiously continue down the corridor casual-like until I make it to the large soundstage. Studio people are milling around the room, and there are four large TV studio cameras along the far wall. I further scan, and there in the center of it all is Micky Dolenz in position behind the drums, while Peter Tork stands near him with a bass guitar strapped on. This sight causes me to stall and drift sideways to the nearest spot in the wings, where I nestle into a corner next to the scene's portable backdrop that is covered in painted balloons. A small black metal box by my feet suddenly splurts out some blow-bubbles, and I jump back. As the bubbles float around me, I take advantage of their cover and quickly scan the room to see if anyone's noticed. That's when I realize I've just planted myself behind Davy Jones, who appears to be waiting for the final touches to be touched before they do a take. He's got on a Vegas lounge singer smoking jacket, and his hair and tan make him look a lot more like Joe Pesci in Martin Scorsese's recent movie *Casino* than sixties tambourine aristocracy.

Suddenly, I've registered on his radar, and I can see he's giving me a wandering once-over from the farthest corner of his eye, then turns attention back toward the pending action. After a few settled-back moments, he begins to quietly hum a tune to himself. His shoulders slack, and then ever so slightly, they begin to switch along as his elbows slightly raise, and the faint hum now turns into words sung just louder that barely audible.

It was "Daddy's Song," originally written by Nilsson and performed by Davy in *Head*. It couldn't be a coincidence that he would see an obvious young sixties-enthusiast "head" in the wings and then sing this song seemingly to himself. It more than succeeds in sedating me and makes me question my mission of bother. I'm going to need to take another drink.

The woman directing calls for a take. The band moves into position and then silence. *BEEP, BEEP, BEEP, BEEP*, and the prerecorded backing track blasts loud as the band goes into miming the song. Instead of the mind-bending four-in-hand double-grip maraca shake-shake assault of the sixties TV show, Davy's only got two maracas in one hand, while in the other he's holding a drumstick and hitting a single electronic drum pad, seemingly trying to "beef it up" for some reason. Hard times for middle-aged maraca players, seemingly. Nobody young had made it cool again yet.

Bubbles keep blowing from near my feet, so I decide to blend in a little more, but as I walk along the set perimeter to get lost in the crew, I realize I'm just putting myself on everyone's radar. Could I be some weirdo with no real business here who's going to try to pull something? Suddenly, the director calls for another take. *BEEP, BEEP, BEEP, BEEP* comes in the count, which gets Mikey going from behind the kit, his vocal track sounding just like he did back in the day when seemingly tapping into his inner Grace Slick, but without all the righteous sixties music gear they had back then, the guitar tone here sounds much closer to grunge, the popular music of these days. Staying relevant. Peter is robot breakdancing, trying to bring the "fun," but it just looks incredibly dorky.

Ondi sneaks a wave to me from behind one of the large studio cameras. She can't make direct contact with me, and rightly so, if they'd like to keep this job for the rest of the day. I go out a side alley door and take a pull off my vodka pint. Getting impatient, David meets me out there. "So, what do you think? Any way we can get you to do something on camera?"

I pull from my vodka again, then peer into the doorway to sneak a peek. The guys are in a slightly anxious in-between-takes limbo. They have to be *on* the moment the director calls "action." Peter is smiling and practicing his robot dance, while Davy trades feet in anticipation. All the cameras are ready. The whole room is now waiting for the director.

"Okay, here we go ... action!" she calls, and as the

playback track begins its beeping count-in, I start strolling off toward the direct center of the shot. I walk right into the middle of everything, stop dead center in front of the band, look both ways like I'm lost, check my imaginary watch, then continue on my way and out of frame. The playback track starts to blast loudly, but the band are all just standing and looking sideways toward me now off camera. The bubble machines stop.

"Cut!"

Now the music stops.

"Get that guy outta here!"

I'm promptly whisked away by be-headsetted dolly-gripping best boys and escorted back though the studio lobby and out into the bright burn of Hollywood's reality studios. Just as I begin mentally reviewing my new empty list of options, Ondi comes out. "Oh my *God*, that was great! Every camera in there just got that! Nobody can figure out what just happened!"

Ondi is taking on, as I'd find she often would, the seemingly ever-present Los Angeles sun in an under tank top and cargo pants, thus creating the original prototype look for the world-adventuring female documentary filmmaker. Kinda like the pregnant redhead character Cate Blanchett plays in Wes Anderson's film *The Life Aquatic*. Come to think of it, during the *Dig!* editing period Ondi was pregnant and still a natural redhead ... and Tara, one of her close friends, who will by then be an ex of Anton's, was by then dating Wes Anderson ... whose next movie became *The Life Aquatic.* Could the Cate Blanchett character be modeled after ... *nahh*, I think I read somewhere that it was Jane Goodall, the woman who lived with and observed The Monkees. I mean the monkeys.

Where was I? Oh yeah. Ondi goes back inside to finish filming The Monkees while I wait inside the SUV with what's left of the vodka. Cheers.

Cursed Cars

Ondi and David arrive at our new BJM band Monkees-style band house in Los Angeles as I make my last-minute adjustments in the bathroom mirror. I've got on tight black boot-cuts over ankle-high Beatle boots, matching turtleneck, and a dark-blue no-name-brand long-collar trucker jacket I'd gotten at Jet Rag over on La Brea. A pair of mirrored faux-Persol Ratti model 23/91 sunglasses rest in the nest on my head. The other guys look cool too, but for the sake of time, just trust me on this.

As Matt and I have sort of doubled up, as you do when you are jail cell roomies, new drummer Brad, who may be trying to punch above his ability level but has hair just like Brian Jones, and Jeff Davies have become a bit of a team lately. When the suggestion of what photo session props to use comes up, they are quick to grab the new sitar replacements, being the coolest looking things to pose with outdoors without a plug. Anton grabs an acoustic guitar while Matt doesn't care, or something.

As we assemble on the front lawn, I decide to copy our single big front yard tree's everyday pose, then Matt follows suit, except he doesn't know the theme I have going with the tree and so goes into a snotty guy slouch thing, while new guy Peter Hayes is officially making it tradition to fade into the background. Leave as little physical evidence behind as possible, seemingly. Oddly, despite knowing this was the big plan today, Sophie has skipped out on the shoot.

Click click. Click click.

We shoot some, and then it's time for a change of concept, and next thing you know, we're all lined up on the aqua-colored stucco porch in *American Gothic* painting position, with Jeff holding garden shears, which I guess is a continuation of this morning's theme. Brad has a hoe, Anton a rake, Matt has a pitchfork, and I, of course, have the shovel. Peter doesn't participate in the props.

Click click. Click click.

Ondi wears a small cowboy hat but wields a big lens, and now they want to go shoot in the nearby LA River here in Atwater Village, where apparently much of its wide concrete channels are currently completely dried up.

Our manager Dave's not here, man, and so we all head for Brad's fifties Ford Thunderbird, when Jeff quickly shouts, "Shotgun!" and I duck in some kind of automatic reflex. Matt climbs in and is immediately stuck in bitch position by Anton and hazy Peter Hayes, unexpectedly both coming in from opposite ways. There's no more room now, and so by default, I'm suddenly the odd man out, and I ride with Ondi and David, which happens often on these types of excursions. Yet no matter how many times it happens, I don't see it coming until it does.

Brad goes into his sneering faces like he always does when driving, starting with his full sneer for the over-the-shoulder reverse out of the driveway model; then it's just a sort of "this stinks" resting face for general forward cruising. I get the feeling it's like even this level of being in situational control comes with a superiority complex, or maybe it's just so that one never gets too comfortable in "his house." Maybe he just hates driving, but I don't really think it's that.

Anton is in good spaces these days, this dimension and otherwise, and so we are once again in a comfort zone where the band will function like a band while he almost takes an observer's position—usually his way of taking a little break while building up reasons over time how and in what ways everyone around him is doing it wrong and will then take charge again. These close little in-between zones are the best, and Matt and I can breathe and laugh easily. Brad, meanwhile, has to work harder at avoiding practicing the drums, despite Anton's wishes that he try to improve, and Jeff looks for avenues to gain ground within the group's pecking order. Not faulting here, it's actually more common than the other with musicians, as well as a needed source for dramas to sprout, if that is your thing. I'm starting to feel a little like a jerk for flirting so much with the smarmy sides of my POVs, but after all, these are my private head thoughts, and in here, nobody knows but me. Plus, Jeff and Brad have instigated these feelings by initially giving me the same kind of deal, but out loud, so yeah, plot twist, and suddenly I'm a nice guy taking the high road.

Unfortunately, this also allows for things like Jeff and what goes on in his live-in closet to start taking another forever. Ondi and David begin to juggle scenarios, entering and exiting the good footage zones, and now cracks are already starting to form in Anton's Zen veneer, now stepping in with suggestions of furtherment in his red peppermint-colored ornate button-up shirt, which will not go on to make his regular wardrobe rotation, unfortunately.

We only need to go four or five blocks to get to the "river" and could actually have walked it San Francisco style, but the car is, in fact, the next prop. We pull up to the cement edge, and it's all very *Repo Man* and *Point Blank* in its sprawling, dried-up, and sunbaked concrete jungle glory. First we pose where we are, around and even on Brad's parked car. Ondi and David are both armed and focused in with wide angles, positioning to get us all in the shot.

Click click. Click click.

Palms sway in the distance as we then all walk down the river's slope and into the center's sprawling emptiness where once was rapid water but is now over it and now not over it. We group pose around the wide empty as the cameras click, when somehow Matt suddenly has a cap gun and is pointing it to his head. It's something that looks oddly natural on him, kinda Jesus & Mary Chain nihilist and also feeds into his familiar defeatist state. Another roll is loaded as our group regroups. Whoever wasn't is by now comfortable with the shoot, and we give the camera more of our true essential selves, some of us better than others.

Click click. Click click.

Later, Greg Shaw seems less than impressed with the day's results, most likely due to the indie music label world's sworn code of penny pinching. Despite not wanting to pay for the pictures, what neither he nor we know is that today we've just shot the shot that will wind up down the road being the flagship advertising image for *Dig!* and to a large degree the band itself, historically speaking. It is also not known that actor Harry Dean Stanton, who's had a film reference in this piece, will be making for a third and in-person appearance at our housewarming party tonight, but then that's a story that's already been told in full … maybe.

* * * *

"It's a lot longer the second time," Matt instructs. "I'll nod when the switch is coming."

"It's full gospel blues," Anton adds. 'Clap hands' ya know?" He put his pick in his mouth and elbow dances a pair of raised claps in the song tempo.

"*Ye*aah …" Matt agrees yet stretches the word out to signify some level of discomfort with having someone else explain a song he feels he's mostly written. We're showing Peter, the new guy, "No Come Down," and the time switch in the song.

"Yeah, I see what you're saying. The first time is just like a little turnaround …" Peter Hayes says while twirling his finger in the air for visual accompaniment. He seems pretty spacy, *like the circles that you find, in the pinwheels of your mind*, but understandably reserved during these too-late feel-out days, or he's just a perma-spacy reserved guy, which would actually be a welcome element to the group. New super-outgoing motivated types always seem to burn out here somehow, finding themselves coming out on the other side of all this as something else.

"Hey, you guys, I'm going to the store," our

reinstated band manager, Dave D, interrupts. "Last call for strings and batteries."

We all look over to him, but no one responds. He then gets two steps out the door, and Matt, Brad, and I all yell "Beer!" somewhat in unison, then it's back to teaching Peter the new song.

"Soo, I'll look for you to signal and then …" His young black curls look like question marks.

"I'll nod," Matt says while nodding to what he's saying but not necessarily demonstrating.

I jump in. "If it helps, when we do it live, I have a tambourine beat that lands in the middle of the two parts. Then everybody comes in again." I like this song despite it being pretty close to something from Spiritualized. Or maybe it just makes me a little uneasy with its lyric of "If I catch up to you, I'm gonna break your skull in two." My right temple twinges for a second.

"He's doing the sixteenth-note thing up until then," Anton adds.

It's Matt's song, so he wants to add the final word on the subject. "Then he switches, and it's after the first beat."

"After the first beat." He's got it now.

"Yes."

"You guys all come in together," I add, just in case.

"Everybody," Matt says, retaking his position of giver of the last word.

Anton puts his pick down on his amp and starts pulling his guitar over his head. "Fuuck, man, it's not rocket science, it's gospel music. I'm gonna smoke." He gets up from the twin reverb amp he's been sitting on and heads for the door, sparking his lighter at the same moment his foot makes its first step outside into the Los Angeles outdoor oven.

"Never mind, I guess," Matt dismisses.

It's getting kind of boring, I have to say, and if this were happening today in the times of smartphones, I'd definitely be pulling mine out right about now.

Anton's head suddenly pokes back through the door, and I shove it back in my pocket fast. "It doesn't mean you guys have to stop!"

"It's fine, we'll come back to it," Matt assures him.

I pull it out again as he continues from outside the room. "I just want to make sure we learn some of the new ones," he sighs, bringing half of his last drag with him. "Okay, here is the song. Brad, we need to talk swing time," he says without breaking momentum while moving toward the kit, where Brad automatically gets up and holds the sticks out. Anton sits behind the kit and breaks into erect Art Blakey posture. "Peter, do you remember this one from the tape we gave you? Will you play this one? Okay, check this out, it swings like jazz," he says before going into a shuffly demonstration. Peter joins in, strumming lightly in a way that's not wholly committing, just in case he's maybe playing it wrong or it feels weird to be playing it by himself in front of Anton. Anton continues to shuffle it along as Brad watches. A moment ago, while sitting behind the kit, he'd had a hard-case air about him, but now he seems more vulnerable somehow, just standing there to the side. He takes a hold of a dangling arm with the other.

Meanwhile, there is no social media yet, so the only

option for this in these birth-of-the-internet days is to use the computers at cafes, but either way, those ran six or seven dollars per hour, and even if you wanted to throw down that kind of money, you'll find the sign-up boards are permanently a mile long with names wanting to continue their "electronic billboard conversations," so I'm just reading entertainment news. Hmm, the *Saturday Night Live* comedian Mike Myers has a new movie out; looks like he's trying to be all sixties or someth—

"Joel!" Anton hollers while standing, and I yank the phone back down from my face like it was trying to fly into my eye or something. "Will you start the song so Brad can see how he comes in?"

I start the single-beat tic-toc, which is my sole part nonstop all the way through.

"Watch," Anton redirects, then stops and counts out loud, "One-two-three-one-two-three-one-two-three-one-two-three," *tatatta-tatatta-tatatta-tat* and back in again. Matt comes in on bass this time, and they plonk, chop, and swing their way toward the next break in the song. This time I fill it in with the tambourine hits and explain as I do, "I do two sets of three in the breaks. Like *tist tist tiss, tist tist tiss*, Anton repeats the military-style drum count-in but stops before going into the song outro. "6/4 jazz," he says, standing up and handing the sticks back to Brad, who's smiling—but it's the wheel-turning kind that goes straight back instead of up, so the bottom teeth are displayed equally with the tops.

Just then, Dave comes back in with plastic shopping bag handles crinkling in that loose way they do when there's nothing heavy like beer in them and announces,

"Hey, I forgot to tell you I heard 'Never Ever' on KXLU yesterday!"

This isn't the first time today that everyone has ignored something Dave has said, so Matt fields it. "Maybe we should rerelease it as a twelve-inch with an added techno beat."

"See? Now you're thinking, Matt," Dave says welcomely. "That's where the ducketts are these days. Just ask Bee-jork or Beyurk or Bjork or whatever."

Matt starts singing, "I can move, move, move any mountain," while pointing alternating forefingers in the air like a happy cowboy.

"Yeah, until you fall off its cliff. Did you hear? That's what happened to their singer, The Shamen guy, *while* they were filming the video to the actual song, man. Or did he drown and people just like to make fun of the lyrics and say he fell off a cliff?"

Brad cuts off the going-nowhere conversation. "Let's do the song."

Dave, *almost* invisibly annoyed, starts in on his customary faux-forgetfulness routine. "Ohh, shiit. Did you guys say you wanted beer? *Oops.*"

Anton sees where this is all going and fully beheads the matter. "C'mon, you guys, quit fuckin' around. Let's do this."

"Fine," Matt says while pushing his glasses all the way back up from where his raving had shaken them down to.

Anton puts his strumming hand to the strings and raises his chin in that expectant look before bringing them down together with the start of the song. After one full guitar progression, I start in on the tambourine, to further set the pace for Brad, and we all take off. Sometimes it feels like rehearsal just goes on and on, and for me, it can be pretty boring stuff, especially when the band is first learning new songs, but hearing this song come together for the first time is the magic stuff serious highs are made of. Luckily, there are no actual cell phones in this reality for me to have at some point during this thought I needed to check it.

These hours-long rehearsals are the centerpiece of our days. Despite there being no question among the neighbors as to which gang of weirdos is banging away in there, we keep the rehearsal room window blinds permanently closed, to keep any visual in-progress a mystery. The downside to this is that nothing else from the world's light palette can mix in with the horrible electric yellow that blasts the room at an optical level of eleven. This musical environment mix of blissful and bunker-like conditions makes the sun and the sky outside all the more necessary, and so the breaks come often. These frequent refreshers serve to stretch the days out long like taffy, sweet with holes that grow and multiply further with the pull.

Everyone is arranged haphazardly out on the grass in front of the house while enjoying some clean air and cigarettes, when an old woman walking by turns her head toward us and complains in that tone that angry old ladies own. "I had to park *way* over there because you guys have so many cars!"

Jeff cheerfully jokes with her, "We're sorry, we actually don't like each other, so we all have to drive separately every time we go hang out somewhere together."

She doesn't seem to care for this answer all too much, and rather than respond, she begins to mutter a droning something-or-other under her breath while simultaneously one-handedly counting fingers with thumb repeatedly. There's an odd rhythm to it all, as if she's performing a ritual or putting some sort of a curse on us or maybe even a combination of the two. I know what odd rhythms look like when I see them, not curse rituals.

"*Seee?*" Dave says once she continues down the sidewalk. "I'm on *her* side. Every time I come home, one of you guys is parked in the driveway or blocking the driveway. There's waaaa— (a portal made of a's opens and we all spiral through its vortex for I don't know how long, could have been days) —aaaaay too many cars around here, man."

One by reckoning ...

Who could forget the pulse-pounding single-sentence explanation from the other book regarding losing the beat-up white Subaru after getting too many parking tickets.

One by expiration ...

A few days later, Brad, Matt, and I are cruising down Glendale Boulevard in Brad's Thunderbird, when suddenly the engine just drops dead.

"*Fuck!*" Brad announces.

"Did the engine just die?" Matt asks from the back seat while darting his head in various alternating opposite directions.

"Yes, the engine's just died," he returns, annoyed. The car goes into a coast as we all turn around to see what's still blazing toward us from behind at the customary twenty-five miles over the 25-mph speed limit. Luckily, despite this being a busy area of strip malls and other Los Angeles what-have-yous, no one is immediately coming, which is good, except now as we slow to a stop on the incline, Brad discovers that the brakes don't work either.

"Welp, the brakes are dead. I guess that's it, guys," he says very matter-of-factly, and we begin to slowly roll backward. It's a six-lane thoroughfare, and as bad luck would have it, we are in the lane closest to the opposite traffic, so Brad will have to coast us over the other two lanes. And here comes the best part—while we roll backward around the oncoming blind curve.

"Fuuck!" Matt says, turning back toward us, no longer wanting to look. His eyes are wide, but his mouth is pushed in tight from all four sides like it's his scared alien impersonation. He's backlit from outside, with a few palms blowing in the distance and the disappearing road lined with car-repair shops, chiropractors, and funeral homes. There'd been free-flowing steady traffic in all directions on this ride so far, and now we're all alone and just waiting for the flying cars to appear into view from around the turn, to deliver the last split-second before we're instantly smash-compacted tight inside this steel trap of vintage cool.

I take a break from this widescreen view of impending death as we continue rolling farther down toward Dead Man's Curve at ten miles per hour, to check Brad's handle on this whole scene. Now *he's* definitely the way you wanna go, a black-leathered elbow jutting back over the seat while one-handed sneer-steering us across the lanes, looking like a Ray Ban-ed Brian Jones with all the defiance of a WWII fighter pilot whose plane is engulfed in flames while crashing straight down with guns a-blazing right through the gates of hell. Now I'm really wishing that I could handle it that way, but I'm feeling more like "X-Files Hollywood" with his *scared gray alien in a Beatles disguise* expression.

As you probably know from the now-omnipresent pageant of spoiler alerts that is the Sundance Grand Jury Prize–winning (by unanimous decision, no less) documentary *Dig!*, we made it. The Thunderbird did not survive.

One by hustle ...

Remember in the other book I don't remember what happened to Peter's van? I still don't, but in any event in the life of a stoned child on Her Majesty's Secret Universe, maybe that old lady *had* cursed us.

The look on Dave's face later that day—leaning up against the back of his van, arms folded and smiling a long one. He'd never have to fight for driveway rights again. His van was sitting square dead center in the driveway, equidistant from the grass on both sides, yet with not a care as to how close or far away from the end of the little driveway. Now that everyone would once again be relying on him as the sole vehicle owner, he was reinstated to his command post in his back-to-fully-operational control freak command center.

How much was he paying that old lady?

I Think That Maybe I'm Dreaming...

"Haay, wanna bite of my Chaaco Taaco?" Jeff offers, smiling with chocolate on his teeth inside smeared red-sticked lips spread across his alabaster face. The corner of my mouth quirks a "No thanks" to this part–kind gesture/part-attempt to enlist me as last-second accomplice in making us wait at this boring gas station for an extra seventeen minutes while he's inside perusing the aisles for every last useless thing on offer, before then spending an additional forever in the bathroom. It was to be expected and had even been joked about as we all first exited our manager Dave D's van, but it was the finale of talking to the faux-interested cashier for an additional four minutes that officially placed him past the point-of-no-return as far as annoying goes. His seemingly genuine obliviousness cuts the shit-giving from Brad in half as Dave D drawls long from the driver's seat like blowing out a gigantic bong hit, "Is everybody heeere?", like somehow he had no reason to know the rest of us have been in here with him the whole time while giving our annoyed commentary and inserting our own dubbed dialogue to the conversation on the other side of the station window glass. Wanting some small grain of control back in my life, I switch with Anton and join Matt in Ondi and David's SUV for the last hour stretch to Monterey.

... I think maybe I dreaming ... Monterey!

I love Eric Burdon and the Animals, especially the period of "San Franciscan Nights" and his complete devotion to psychedelia and the hippie dream. The song "Monterey," with its over-the-top enthusiasm, ultimately sounded a little uncool and goofy to me, but that's also kinda what's good about it, if you know what I mean. Still, listening to it now sitting next to Matt back on the road en route to our appearance at what is being billed as "The 30th Anniversary of The Monterey Pop Festival," it's currently taking on a whole next level of meaning. In 1967, The Monterey Pop Festival was the first rock-and-roll festival in history. Up until then, rock bands could only play jazz, folk, or blues festivals, and while Monterey Pop was still both genre- and internationally diverse, it was centered mainly around the new psychedelic rock.

I gaze out the window at the otherworldly-looking coastal purple, orange, and green beach foliage lining both sides of the highway that was cut right through the sandy slopes. Matt nudges me on the shoulder and passes back our "sneaky pete" pint of vodka that we're sharing stealthily, so as not to alert David that we're risking his driver's license by having an illegal open container in the vehicle. This and it being too early for the new day's disappointments to be discovered, especially being confined here inside a vehicle driving down the highway where you can't get to most of them, Matt is joining me for a good mood. The morning buzz kickstarts from the tummy, and we begin to exchange endearment-fueled parodies of Eric Burden and his apparent difficulty to comprehend the high level of magic surrounding what he had experienced down in Monterey.

Once in Monterey proper, we pull up to the festival grounds entryway and see Dave D in his van with the rest of the BJM gang parked and waiting by the Old West–style welcome sign. The prearranged plan is to drive in together, but after hello waves are acknowledged, Anton suddenly gets out and comes up to Ondi's open window.

"You know, they wanted the Beatles to headline the original, but Paul McCartney sent Jimi Hendrix instead, and they're like '*Who?*' because nobody over here had heard of him yet. Paul basically had to tell them it was happening because they wanted to draw the biggest crowd possible, and nobody in America knew who Hendrix was yet. The promoters were the people who originally started hippie capitalism and kicked off the whole 'Summer of Love' thing, and suddenly, like a million kids came from everywhere to Haight Street, and then they were like, 'Oh, shit.'"

"Gimme one second, Anton. I want to get the camera out." Ondi smiles while leaning into a reach.

I take this cue and jump out to ride in the band van, while Anton climbs into the SUV. Matt follows, and together we cram into the can of baked band. Dave D takes one more toke and leads the convoy of two up and under the canopies of green trees to the VIP route security checkpoint.

This is my first outdoor festival performance of any kind, and I get a druggy-like tingle inside as we begin driving along the "ARTIST ONLY" perimeter route toward the big stage where it all happened—the stage where Jimi and The Who made their US premieres, the stage that served as the launchpad for the Summer of Love and all the psychedelic rainbow vapor trail that followed it.

I think maybe I'm dreaming... Monterey!

We approach the rear of the massive stage, but instead of stopping, Dave D passes it by and continues on. He points to the grounds map as he drives and says, "The map says we're on the stage that's coded blue. This one's red."

Huh?

Without an immediate explanation available, I take a drift to skip stones across the ponder... I didn't know that about Paul and Jimi and the capitalist side of the hippie movement. It's also likely what probably popped the black light idea bulb over Eric Burdon's head to do his recap theme. *Now! You can be there too! Buy the album and be IN!* "The dream" used from both ends to make one very large loaf of bread made of many slices, with which many sandwiches were made. Not to totally poo-poo the pomp and circumstances of success, but at the same time, while sitting here staring out the window at all the vacancies, I'm wonderi—

"Weeeeeeeeeeeird," Dave D unrolls like a long Persian hallway rug. "This thing's supposed to have opened up a couple of hours ago. Where is everybody?"

He's right, this place is dead, and the few who are here seem to be walking around in zombielike lonely confusion. The vendors are vending to no one. The various wooden picnic bench areas and food shacks are empty yet must be stocked with enough supplies for thousands. There's so much more activity going on behind the scenes, or rather normal activity, that compared to the sprawling uninhabited spectator areas, it's almost like a large event set up in reverse. Now, this is a good excuse to get fucked up again. Always gotta find the positive angle.

We finally make it all the way out to where we can see the second stage off in the distance. As we grow nearer, Jeff recognizes some friends near our vastly smaller stage.

"No *waay!* Look, yooguuys, there's Phil!"

"Oh, wow!" Brad reinforces as he stiffens to periscope position.

Jeff is already crawling over everyone in his path from the back of the van, then enthusiastically slides the side door open and jumps out like it's a helicopter scene from *Mission: Impossible*. He hurdles off of the slow-rolling van and goes flying down the foot-and-a-half drop to land feet first on the grass. Our only group of local Monterey friends see him coming, and all faces light up. Especially Phil, who runs to meet him halfway. Everyone loves Jeff, especially those who do not have to clock in hours of portable waiting room time. Even those brief encounters with redneck gas station clerks or grouchy diner waitresses played out with them giving in to his unique brand of aloof, childlike, effeminate ways. He had that otherworldliness sheen that many from "normal" society couldn't wrap their head around, yet instead of defaulting to norms like contempt, would just accept him and the experience while still sneering at the rest of us.

For further crowd attendance, there is only a smattering of hodge-podgers around the stage, including a customary psychedelic Santa Claus type right in the front, which is a standard-issue California outdoor stage mascot.

Somewhere in the Bay Area, there must be a rent-a-hippie holdover service, which if there is, would have cost about the same as the entire advertising budget spent on the rest of the festival. Apparently, the promoters had only sprung for a single quarter-page, one-time ad in last week's *San Francisco Guardian* paper. That was the whole ad campaign. If you didn't happen to pick up that free paper last week and see the right page, then you had no idea that this huge event was taking place. Turns out, all in all, only about 150 people experienced this combination of events, who are now spread slim-chance thin around the entire fairgrounds.

The SUV pulls up behind us, and Matt and I begin goofing large for the cameras. Lessons are being doled out fast as to what kind of relationship each of us wants with Ondi and David's all-seeing camera eyes. Anton's and mine had already been established in Portland. Jeff, who it must be said would be very serious competition for the most fun on-camera personality, has already chosen to mostly withdraw from being filmed as permanent policy after seeing the look on Ondi's face while he played his spoon in front of her. Peter was seemingly just the new kid and relegated to a corner unless there were some master-and-student moments with Anton to capture. Brad, like me, was born on *A Hard Day's Night* and also rose to the on-camera occasions, unless he was internally dealing with the hard day's realities of which band we were *really* in and the crosshairs that were permanently fixed on the drummer's stool. When Matt wasn't playing along with us, he would weirdly be the most honestly natural. He'd finally found his ear for his fountain of ever-flowing grievances, which I in no way want to imply were invalid, because they were usually thought out and frequently spot-on, but being right, even really, really, really right, oftentimes doesn't help the situation.

To be fair, I'd actually found my own sense of solace in becoming his private confidant in a complainer's secret underground movement. Like Dean and our head-shaking, Matt and I practiced morale-solving through problem-spotting. Why is complaining so satisfying? Despite this, none of us even knows where to begin with the disappointments today because the botch level of this entire festival is so grandiose. To single any one thing out would carry all the importance of holding a match to the sun or a drop in the ocean.

By the time we get off stage, all of the free beer behind our stage is gone, which is one of the problems with having friends, and so Matt and I become curious as to what's going on across the fairgrounds at the Royal Trux performance on the main stage. Specifically, will our artist wristbands get us into that backstage area where we can pilfer booze to our livers' discontent. I've heard this band before, and although they're coming form a lot of the places I like, it's not really my thing, but then, I can also be kinda music snobby, which is another thing among my many more positive other things.

After a long, somewhat sobering march, we find that in accordance with keeping in the spirit of the entire day, with this new modern bummer version of the Monterey Pop dream, we cannot. Now, so far away from the others, we decide to head out into the humongous seating area, where a life-changing crowd would usually go, and position ourselves in a row close to the stage but off to the side. I count fifty-two chairs with bodies and 8,448 empty ones. The band doesn't seem to be happy with all of this either, by the way the singer delivers her vocals extra raspy, or maybe that's regular raspy, but it seems like extra. She prowls the stage, seemingly looking for the alternate reality we'd also tried to spot earlier.

We're floating on a vast sea of seats surrounding us in all directions. They are the metal fold-out ones and are tied together at the legs in sets of four like a group hostage situation. This is probably to prevent them from being used for something other than sitting, like throwing, and if the idea was to keep these tied together to stop them from being thrown, in this scenario, the empty chairs are instead now empty couches, which Matt and I begin to fling freely into the air. The nearest concertgoer isn't seen for miles around, and so we hurtle the bound and gagged chair captives to and fro with glee. It's a groovy kind of satisfaction that delivers us from frustration in the way only public destruction can.

We each get about four metal skeleton couches launched before the rented doughboys in gray move in. Huffing up a sweat on the walk over, they finally get to perform a duty today by each gently taking an arm of Matt's and mine and walking us down the aisle. We go quietly, smiling at each other in the knowledge that at least we'd stood up together and fought back against all the disappointments, just like in the sixties.

I think maybe I'm dreaming ...

Three-Button Tinfoil Mod Suit

a a h — a h h...

The Brian Jonestown Massacre are on their way to the UK for the very first time, where currently our Virgin Atlantic flight is making the right turn at Greenland.

"Dean, I think all these stewardesses are in love with you," Jeff observes while tilting his head to Dean sitting next to him.

"I noticed." He's joking, but we've all noticed it.

Anton stops one who's just passing by, "Miss, I think you've mistakenly seated me in the big ape section," he says, looking pleased with himself and grinning widely at me. She looks us over and nods slightly, kind of seeing what he's saying, which I sort of get, I guess, but she doesn't know how to respond, so she just continues on.

"Man, whose side are these people on?" I complain with an amused head shake. We're all jazzed on being en route to England and buzzed on the pre-dinner cocktails and dinner wine.

"Travis, they're playing the Spice Girls movie," Matt offers to our guitar tech and "fifth Beatle." His hand is doing this side-of-mouth thing, like it's a wing, something to visually give his words some extra carry across the aisle.

"I know," he returns in his already-familiar amused-with-slight-embarrassment chuckle combo. "I can watch it at least three times before we land." He's actually not kidding but is also our odd-man in and will be under our inside-out umbrella for many years to come.

Matt and I both simultaneously hit the call button again.

"Hi, what can I get you?" the approaching stewardess asks, knowing by now it's about more booze. We order another round, and she leaves.

"Coffee, tea, or me?" Jeff says, smiling from the seat separation in front of us. It takes about five minutes on the road to start the groaning contests, so by this point it's almost like a twenty-year-old Johnny Carson episode that can't be turned off.

"That was the famous loose stewardess catchphrase in the seventies, when everybody flying airplanes were on quaaludes," he adds.

"The pilots?" Dean asks.

"Yes. Even the pilots. They all had big Burt Reynolds mustaches, gold chains, and smoking cigarettes. They even had guns up in the cockpit too. Still do."

"In the cockpit? Is that safe?"

"Yes, but not if you just whip it around all willy-nilly, because if it went off, that would create a serious release of cabin pressure." Then switching from regular animated voice to "normal person" voice, "I'm sorry, officer, I was just cleaning it, and it went off."

I'll let you in on a little secret. When we're not trying to kill each other on stage, we're usually unconsciously still trying to stupid each other to death. It's a questionable close-quarters coping mechanism that will suffice for now, until I realize through subsequent lineups that it's forever.

"I'll bet, huh, huh." Dean chuckles. He turns back our way to see Anton, me, and Matt all performing synchronized silent-grin judging head shakes.

"*What?*" He would like to know, with a three-way split of amused, annoyed, and guilty kind of look that signifies he already knows very well "what."

Matt fields it. "How did we get in a band with Beavis and Butthead?" It would have been an even more perfect rip if Jeff hadn't just had his braces removed from his teeth.

The stewardess brings our drinks plus a pair of spare minis of the same to save herself the next trip in twenty minutes from now, but that is actually the amount of time it will take for her to learn this trick does not work. From here, we switch topics to the pros and cons of Zen, I think it was, or something else similarly esoteric and profound. Over the next few hours, I forgo sleep as the cocktails continue to go down me until the unstoppable free drinks meet the immovable Customs desk.

There are bodies everywhere, the battlefield aftermath of a massive and long war waged against boredom. All around me are discarded blankets, lost pillows, unwatched screens playing on to the temporary dead. People lie still in every imaginable position within the fiendishly forced combination conditions of horizontal and vertical simultaneously, all in some varied but similar unnatural position. The lucky ones are lying over others, while some are half in the aisle, none looking peaceful as the strained looks of "sleeping" faces suffer on. I too must now join them, for no one can escape the inevitable. I give the darkness one last stare goodnight as my eyes slowly close, and I switch over to inside-my-head darkness.

Suddenly, a blasting white light screams silently from above as if I've just woken up on the roof of a supermarket in Sistine Chapel painter's position. I open my eyes to the captain's wake-up call and meandering summary of what's not going on and that we'll be arriving in London soon.

With the lights up again, I can see the others on the plane, and I have to wonder if they are even the same people from before. When I imagine giant slumber parties with free booze that can soar above the clouds en route to swinging-mad-for-it places like London, my mind is blown over what a crummy party it is up here. Turns out the jet set wasn't all it was cracked up to be. At least not anymore.

Then, ten tons of instant comedown in the short gallows walk they call "departing," and stumbling out of what had just been nighttime interior into the broad, bright morning daylight was like walking into a microwave oven with a tinfoil suit on.

Suddenly, and just like that, here I was, alone in this human maze of disheveled misery that is the Heathrow Customs Control counter line after what must have been at least fifteen gin-and-tonics, many of which were doubles. Now they were all making a mass exodus out of my body through my pores, traveling by fumes like exorcised ghosts fleeing for better hosts.

Where had all the good-timers gone? Booze had pulled its masterstroke heist job of my trust through that last glass, and in actual fact, everything would not be all right. Forty-five minutes more of slow-motion battle between inner and outer misery ownage rights, and there was still no sign of my people. They must have gotten so far ahead that they were already through and smoking, hairing-of-the-dog, eating jolly good goods, the lot.

Finally my turn comes to approach the bench. I put what is left of my speaking capability on alert and hand my passport to the agent with the eye contact and waving finger. He's a friendly-looking English gentleman of about my age.

"Purpose of your visit?" he asks casually.

"My band is playing two shows here in London," I say, tipping the wink while hopefully not tipping over.

This triggers a tenth-of-a-second full-service once-over, then he looks down to my passport and flips a few pages of stampless. "May I see your work permit, please?" he instructs.

What's a work permit? I suddenly wonder. "Um, nobody gave me a work permit."

He cocks his head like maybe I'd just turned into some other kind of species, then his tone suddenly goes up about five notches while his vibe goes down twenty. "*Roight!* What d'you *mean* you don't have a work permit? Okay, what you are saying is, that you've come here to work and you don't have a *work permit?*"

Wait, is he saying that playing gigs *is work?*

Sometime later, after finally getting sprung from passport immigration jail, I make it to London, where while shopping for new boots, I literally run into one Bobby Gillesp— Oh, yeah, you've already heard this one before. The next day, we're off to London Bridge, where the Beefeaters roam wild, to get some of that "Yanks running amok in jolly ol' effect" for the press back home. It's also time to reinstate my intoxicated state, and now I've got Matt to recruit to my cause. Thankfully, it's just one of those days, and next our crew is cabbing over to where a BBC Radio crew is waiting for the "essential three" (record label's words, not mine) at, of all places, a pub, where we pitch pints and quip quotes into microphones.

That night, we play The Monarch Club. I find it takes a long time to get to the club because under bar crawl rules, I am only able to proceed further in about ten-foot increments. Even though it's a small, junky dive in Camden Town, it's just a pint glass throw away from the fabled British rock cathedral that was originally a train roundhouse, The Roundhouse. This is where in 1967, the Beatles performed the obscure piece "Carnival of Light" thirty years ago for the Million Volt Light and Sound Rave, and where we will also play in just a short twenty years, making it a total of fifty years of relative relations with the Beatles' career, side by side, bound forever, I'm pretty sure. The show goes great, I should think, but then when I gig, I can do a lot of booze, and then there's perhaps maybe some random irregular regular what-have-yous, possibly, and then I stage-meditate within the blaring stillness.

Me and my twin hangover from yesterday go on a Beatles tour. I know, it's dorky, and that's why I snuck out of the hotel early and alone because I didn't feel like hearing it from the others, but it gets me to where I want to go, and someone else does all the thinking while I can keep my brain safe in my new flight bag–cum man purse case for my mind. Besides, it's not like I can just call some kind of super information center from say one of the red payphone booths and find out all the exact addresses of all the historical points of Beatles interest mapped out with directions. I suppose I could go to a library or something, find some books on the Beatles, and hope they've included addresses, then find them all on a tourist map and figure out the directions, or I can just join the other twenty people in paying the friendly nerd-dude-bloke to lead the way.

It is also still raining from yesterday as he first takes us to the old Apple Records office, where the famous rooftop concert happened. As the tour guide relays history we all know, our group looks up toward the top of the building, but as expected, we can't see what the roof looks like from down here. Then we all go to Paul's current business offices, where we don't catch him riding a bike to work or taking a smoke break out front or anything. Then we walk to some questionably interesting remodeled closed doors and street corners where things used to be, until finally the Tube station that takes us over to St. John's Wood and Abbey Road Studios.

Then it's Tube-beer-beer-Tube-Tube-beer back to the hotel to meet the guys in the lobby. The front desk clerk, who is currently doubling as bartender for us, sadly doesn't know, or at least pretends not to know, what we are talking about when asked which room Bowie and Jagger supposedly "made it" in back in the seventies. Regardless, he's still our favorite person in the world right now, and anyway, sometimes it's best if a musician's lore is left a mystery.

Uh, where was I?

Oh yes, despite hard-earned victories like finally getting to come to London, drama was always lurking just around the corner, and by now Matt and Anton's kitchen battle BJM break-up was only a few weeks away.

Suspicious Mind Stubble

Anton, Jeff Davies, and Dean Taylor all have bad habits going again in time for what is our first post–evil mustache, mind-control full US tour, our first "real" US tour, with a real budget, a competent tour manager, and an album going up the indie charts. The plan, as you can plainly see, was foolproof, and so by the time we'd gigged our way to New York City, we were a touring machine which now found itself barreling down the road so wildly that I had to begin self-preparation for the possibility of us just blasting through the guardrail and off the high bridge, back down to where we'd started, now as burnt and bent-up wreckage. Maybe inside I already know the brakes have gone.

Starting at eight in the morning, the witching hour for out-of-town partying bands visiting New York, the whole group, which included Matt's recent replacement, Charles Mehling, new drummer Billy Pleasant, and our TVT PR reps Jason and Nadine, are all climbing out of two cabs in front of a medium-fancy Italian joint on the Upper West Side of Manhattan.

Once assembled in front of the restaurant, we meet the director and the host of the new VH1 music magazine program called *Rock Candy*, but what's suddenly more interesting to me than the fact that they are filming a piece on us here today is what's happened to Anton's sideburns.

He's shaved them off since I saw him last night, when we played the East Village dive bar the Continental Club. It's one of those places from the seventies music scene that in the seventies, everyone you can imagine from New York in the seventies played.

Now, on closer inspection, not only are his kindred sidies-in-arms gone, but the usual vibe of the rest of the guy is as well, as if some sort of Sampson situation is in effect. The note to self reads: *Shaving off your sideburns has a big effect on energy levels. Avoid doing this.* Then I find out from Dean in hushed undertones that the three of them had done their last bit of stuff last night, and the phone number they'd been given to get more isn't picking up, so now they were all sick.

Strangely, the label giving us the freedom to be anti–music establishment revolutionaries as a marketing strategy was not selling records in this end-of-nineties return to punkless and Britpop-less popular culture climate, and so, maybe not so strangely, apparently TVT's plan B had become selling us off as crazies using Ondi's footage from the first cursed tour as evidence to back up the case.

We're not let in on the joke that we're the joke of the show's predetermined outcome, and the plan is to keep it that way by sequestering each of us away one by one for individual interviews, while the rest are kept in the restaurant bar corner until it's our turn to be called over. To us, everything seems normal enough in that pre–doctor's appointment waiting room form-filling-out way, and we are excited to be doing a TV music channel profile with the added bonus act of helpful assistance from concerned parties. Except that's not what it is. I mean, we're a band, and bands are asking to be exploited, but laughing at dysfunctional, addiction-prone people while dangling a carrot of healing in front of them comes from the same place as Hitler's mustache when you think about it. Which is to say it's the not-good of all not-goods of looks in the evil mustache department.

Up-and-coming comedian and the squarest-looking dude on Earth, which is saying a lot when it's true, Jim Gaffigan is the host of our segment. I talk my answers Zen hip, and Dean outwardly doesn't want to be there, but that's okay if you're good looking. Jeff can ponder 'til the pond dries up, but when Anton isn't able to be Anton, then the headshrinkers start filling up the shrunken-head pot with luxury mineral water.

Band, TVT, and VH1 crew all head over to the psychiatry office of Dr. Cox, whose specialty happens to be addiction. How much did TVT tell this guy? His spacious office is on the upper east side of a large building on the Upper West Side, right across the street from Central Park. He's a sedate dude in that classic shrink way, with enough cushy leather furniture to accommodate an entire band. Unfortunately, they are not of the traditional "Tell me about your mother" leather chaise style but are rather just regular brown couches like the one your mother has. They circle the room like wagons, except all facing each other for an in-fight.

We're not such super-rich crybaby rock stars like his regular clients, Aerosmith, R.E.M., and Bon Jovi, who have unlimited funds to spend on trying to figure out how they can still be in the same room together without puking so they can keep making more millio— I mean, music. In the defense of Dr. Cox, he also seems to not be privy to the comedic angle of the piece and is not playacting this situation beyond his current life-shtick of being a "rock-and-roll psychiatrist."

The session is actually going well, I suppose, in that nobody is arguing, but that's mostly because most of us are "sick." Charles hasn't been around long enough to become physiologically damaged by all this yet, and I don't have much to get off my chest other than having slight abandonment issues because nobody seems to care whether or not I could go for a beer right about now. Dean, Jeff, and Anton all sit on the same couch, which is now the real waiting room couch for waiting for a phone call. Each is hoping the delivery guy will hear the answering machine message left with Dr. Cox's address.

"And how did that make you feel?"

Jeff knows he needs to respond quickly if he is going to keep hold of the room "Amm, it made me feel baad." Of the three, Jeff is the most experienced in dealing with the other internal brand of bad they are all currently feeling together, and he is taking advantage of this opportunity to address long-unspoken issues held by many a BJM member, both past and present, that otherwise wouldn't have a professional on hand who is supposedly being allowed to do something about it. I watch and feel happy for him to get his moment but also wonder why he can't see he's surrounded by fronts on all fronts.

Then the missing junk delivery guy calls from down in the lobby. Slumping postures perk up as if a nurse is

suddenly announcing on the intercom *Medication time ...*
medication time ... and we all once again find ourselves in
One Flew over the Cuckoo's Nest territory. Dean goes
downstairs. A few minutes of Dr. Cox later and we hear
him reenter the office hallway and straight into the
connecting bathroom. Success. Anton and Jeff remain in
perched perfect posture position.

Suddenly, the office door opens, and Dean comes
back into the room with a new unmissable inner glow on
the same level as Julie Andrews suddenly spinning in
circles to the title song from *The Sound of Music.* The
feeling is a real good one that requires an act to disguise,
and so he returns to his spot on the couch and crosses his
legs as to stop the music. He then rejoins the room's
seriousness and pretend-seriousness. Now it's Anton's
turn, which is not to respond to Jeff's fresh points but
rather to go see what Dean's stashed for them in the
bathroom. Soon enough he comes bursting back in with
all the internal intent of Gene Kelly swinging around the
room in a dance routine from *Singin' in the Rain.* Dr. Cox
is in the middle of giving Jeff more positive band
relationship advice that will never work on the other side
of that office door, while Anton sits back down calmly and
relaxed, but with one toe still tapping rapidly in imminent
jailbreak timing.

Next, it's Jeff's turn in the seemingly more effective
healing room, and by now I'm just watching that office
door to see what's going to come back in next. He takes a
few minutes more than the others, but soon enough, he
reappears with inner posture as if being the lead in *Swan
Lake*. So fragile like a fawn, yet sturdy as a birch tree,

with toe tips on pointe, elongated drooping expression with chin down and arms overhead in vertical Jesus fish-head position. I'm positive I can hear the main theme to the ballet gently flowing from the intercom as he scuttles across the carpet and back onto the couch.

Anton's "on" switch is suddenly flipped back to its usual position, and he's now bursting with ideas. "Let's go to the park for ice cream!" he declares, and we all nod, slightly confused at first, but then enthusiastically after, realizing the idea's added accouterment of getting out of this place. We stride out onto the Manhattan sidewalk and across the street into Central Park. Spotting an ice-cream cart, the camera peoples heave-ho onto shoulders and conjoin heads to watch us form our new happy place line to order children's treats. I'm actually not a huge frozen-things guy, so for the sake of good TV, I pick the craziest-looking picture on the cart's front advertising menu, which is a type of red, white, and blue ice rocket ship called an Astro Pop. It's just okay.

As we pull up at Coney Island High on Saint Marks Place for soundcheck, the same club where we'd gotten head-shaked by Joey Ramone, we see our drummer, Billy, waiting outside. We're all climbing out of the taxi van when Anton suddenly declares that we will all be required to wear all white for the show tonight. The whitest shade of pale I've brought with me from California is dark chocolate, and now suddenly the pressure is on to come up with a new outfit before we play in just a few hours. Tonight's New York show's a big event sponsored by TVT, so they can show off their new prize pony Pegasus, The Brian Jonestown Massacre.

Billy's already wearing close-enough-to-the-right-fade Levi's. In some conspiracy circles, it is believed that a drummer's pants don't really exist (they do), but regardless, he's the first runner-up on the convenience roulette wheel, and all he needs to do is pull out a white T-shirt from his bag. Jeff looks down to check himself and is pleased to find he's already wearing all white. He smiles in surprised, proud delight before giving the rest of us whiteless wonders an amused snicker. Our tour manager, Brad, offers Charles his hotel bedsheets to wear as a toga, which in the end only happens in this mental image. I, on the other hand, suddenly need to embark on a solo mission to find white stitching that suits my make and taste. For some reason, someone suggests that I get on the subway up to Midtown, and not knowing any better, I do.

I get off at *Lexington, one two five* ... and I know soon some of us will be waiting for the man for real again, because that's just how that stuff works. Meanwhile, in fashion news, "heroin chic" is very much the thing here now for the designers and those who want to join the new faux-nod-out sect. Even our old friends the Dandy Warhols had jumped on the junkie-culture-as-news bandwagon. For some reason, mass culture was embracing the junkie lifestyle look as an in-trend, and big money was being made by fashion designers and the entire entertainment industry, basically off the image off of *dopers, man.*

To each their own, I say, but even ol' Frankenstein never did figure out how to acquire a second backup Frankenstein suit, and this is all gearing up to be a repeat performance, as once again "the daily special" somehow keeps making it back onto the chalkboard menu every day, making it just another menu item under the guise of being "special" in order to fool the tourists. In reality, the "gritty seventies" New York had been stolen in a land grab long ago by big business, and with it went the rest of it, except for those few who survived with enough left to merit bringing the subject back up every few years.

Suddenly, it feels like I'm being slapped across the face with a full-grown cold turkey as I see a gigantic billboard across the street of the famous close-up of John Lennon and Yoko Ono during their "Bed-in for peace" protest, currently being reappropriated as a Macintosh computer advertisement urging the product consumer to "Think Different." They'd gone for the almighty music jugular that is the Beatles in its first move, and hey, why not? The peace movement of the sixties and seventies wasn't, in the end, a big seller like these computers are, which to this breed of humans justifies its actions. I stare at the billboard in disbelief and realize that there are no "good guys" in *Revenge of the Nerds*.

It's like a Beastie Boys–themed Disneyland in this part of New York, so I call the TVT offices for local vintage intel. Nadine hips me to a place that apparently is the biggest vintage denim store in New York City. I go down to Greenwich Village, and once inside the place, it's like a cathedral of denim. A *Hansel and Gretel* fairytale house made of dungarees in all shapes and colors. I peruse, already knowing I'll be able to score here many times over, and yet I am annoyed at the situation. The one thing that I just can't stand is being told what to wear. Especially if it is white. I am especially not going the go-to guru chil' psych flowing cottons of white path, and I plan to mix it up with my own combination of gear. I push hanger for about ten minutes, and then it begins to click. Once it does, the outfit quickly reveals itself to me from within the racks in the experimental formula of vintage sixties deadstock women's button-front flares and a crisp Harrington "Steve McQueen" jacket. It's technically off-white, but nobody tells me what to do.

With mission accomplished, I'm soon bouncing my way back up the subway station steps and into a horizontal cruise along the sidewalks of Saint Marks Place. On the corner, I'm sucked in by a sunglasses store and blown back out wearing some white-frame eye bubbles to round out my white wares. Once back inside the club, the band is still sound checking, so I quickly B-side-step up to the dressing room and change into what are, for me, my first ever stage clothes. The rest of the band are all in white now, and I join them on stage. I feed my mic a couple of shakes before visually addressing the room with my new ivory duds. We find ourselves forming a mutual appreciation society, and it's then I suddenly learn that there is actually a *really* cool reason why we are all wearing white tonight. Anton's idea isn't just a redo of whatever the old white "come when I call" reasons were. It's a new white-wearing concept, and the plan is to have a projector at the back of the club projecting trippy light images, not on a screen behind us, but *on us.* We ourselves were to be the film screen made of human bodies. *Oh!* Now I've got the white idea.

An hour later, the venue is filling up. TVT Records president Steve Gottlieb arrives and, in a display of solidarity, is debuting his new sideburns. While territory-wise they span the same amount of face real estate as Anton's and mine, it looks like he'd only gotten the idea in the shower this morning, as at the end of the day, they are just very short five o'clock shadow stubble. Still, I don't want to undersell them because technically, it's now four hours after five o'clock, and the day ended around then as well, so a more accurate stubble measurement would be slightly longer, like nine o'clock shadow. The important thing is he seems pretty stoked on this wild move of his, and the least I can do is nod in genuine approval. Regardless, I know enough about life by now to keep my eyes peeled for any suspicious-behaving facial hair, even stubble, especially because this is the exact location spot that I'd noticed the phenomenon the first time around. Either way, you all know what I'm referring to, so I don't have to explain all the ins and outs of the situation again.

Despite a ceremonious air brought to the occasion, by of all unintentional things, hired hippie flower girls wearing white, replete with orchid wreaths, passing out long-stem white roses, pretty much exactly like the Mansonettes at said mustache's execution, tonight will be one of "those" nights. First there are gear problems, followed by the light show projector somehow now being busted, rendering our white clothes just white clothes. When things or people aren't working correctly, Anton tends to take the mic more between songs, which usually splits the audience into two factions, the ones who are interested in whatever the band has to present as honest expression that night and those who were here armed with the dream of being able to bust out the negatives, especially when it's a music muscle showcase. We do indeed give them an excuse to take the night off early, regardless of whether we might regain the chance to change the vibe back over to familiar and "correct" live music experience protocols. Even though we know we have great songs, we're not "playing the game right," and the room goes half empty midway through, or maybe I should say remains half full, which is a typical boozer's positive-glass thinking that I also try to apply to all my life view measuring cups.

The reviews have been proclaiming for years now that on occasion, we are either the most amazing thing ever or a "disaster," though I've never recognized any shows to be as such at the time. At least that I remember that way, when I find my head on the public execution block and *chop!* goes my head, which then rolls across the floor, looks back at my body, and says, "Not to worry, folks! Just a flesh wound, no problem!" *Glug glug glug, shake shake shake* ...

Genesis P-Orridge is waiting for us at the top of the backstage stairs wearing Brian Jones's actual pinstripe suit that he had worn to his 1967 drug bust court case, the event that had officially started his downfall. Genesis has accessorized this celebrity estate auction find with a silver bob wig in the Brian style. My approach triggers a wide, almost maniacal smile that frames a full-mouth metallic grill of sharpened pointy teeth. It's too late to turn back now, and I'm glad, as we officially meet after he'd first seen us play at The Trocadero Transfer now three years ago, when I'd helped Anton lug that heavy B3 organ up the stairs. He thought the show tonight was fantastic.

The music climate of the day is paved with many miles of brand-new bad road, and the current "Alternative Rock" top ten chart reads like the DJ playlist for Satan's elevator operator. The countdown of soundtrack songs for each of the nine descending planes to hell reads as thus: Wallflowers, Third Eye Blind, Dave Matthews, Eve 6, Goo Goo Dolls, Semisonic, Fastball, Everlast, and Stone Temple Pilots. That is the American music world outside of our van that still invades our inner world through the radio speakers, and "Bittersweet Symphony" is only one song.

The 6th Chamber of Guitar Center

Anton and I were walking down Vestal Avenue, back from the little grocery and liquor store in our new Echo Park neighborhood of Los Angeles. Normally our large four-bedroom BJM house slash professional home recording studio on a hill would be stocked with the food basics and booze from the store until the next time the kitchen would magically refill, as it somehow always did. How I don't know, but on the regular occasions the wine supply would run out, we'd make the trek down the hill to LG Market on Echo Park Avenue.

These missions also served, I suppose, as a double unspoken purpose of momentarily clearing the head during hours-long recording sessions or whatever else life was. There is no cable television, the greatest of all distractors, yet we did have a big box of a junker in the back bedroom where Dean had once lived, back when along with Matt there was most of the band residing here and not just Anton and me. But it could only get two or sometimes three channels and always filtered by varying levels of static snowing on the PBS station or otherwise desperate programming.

Anton has on his brown leather calf-high bohemian boots, which he's got white 501 jeans tucked into, a form-fitting white Mexican shirt with an ornate blue rose motif vining around a tunic-style collar and down the front

122

closure, replete with side vents at the hips. It's one I'd picked out for him when he'd told me to "Go to the vintage store and pick out some white clothes for the photo shoot." It was annoyingly a bit too tight for me, these days, but not for him, and so I grabbed it, while I had to settle for a simpler style of more straight-ahead Mexican button-up dress shirt, but nevertheless, was colorlessly compliant.

As much as I appreciated his concept, while not really fully understanding what was behind it, wearing all white with nary a black shade on my body took me out of my own natural selections, and I just couldn't sit comfortably in my own skin during the shoot. Anyway, back at the pulse-pounding walk home from the liquor store, ours is a slightly disheveled suburban neighborhood, with almost every house's front yard bulging with bushy, unkempt yard shrubbery coming up from each of the individual plots of land and then further out into the sidewalks. As we get closer to home, things thin out some, with skinny palms rising high into the sky as we make our way under the bright sun and over cracked concrete sidewalks.

Despite this being a serious upgrade in the character department from our last band pad in Atwater Village, mostly boring-looking houses and modern-ish cars line in rows, while the overabundance of telephone poles casts a network of black wires that zig and zag above us. Still, the neighborhood's overall Latin flare lends it an air that one could effortlessly get very used to, but *transitory* has become religion for us by now, and I don't expect or even want it to ever stop until we get "There."

Where "There" is I think I know, despite its complete

and total unknowingness, but regardless, the war rages on to get "There." Until then, this is about freedom through the music and not the fame and the money and the stuff. Well, enough money to live it up some and be able to continue creating, but not so much to be morphed into a millionaire businessman. Not the way I see it anyway. The way I see it, it's an undeniable thing for nine out of ten of my music heroes that the vast wealth and success simply did not allow for the person they were that first got them "There" in the first place. The race has been won, the war is over, but then what if inside we're all still exactly who we were before? Then what? The more I think about it, another feeling is growing inside of almost never wanting to get fully "There." The uneasy thought of having finally ended the grand adventure and put the Holy Grail above my bed. "There 'There' is, as you can see by it hanging there." Then, "Next."

Next?

Unlike the movies, even documentaries, there is no ending, happy, sad, cliffhanger, French film-style, or otherwise, of anyone's story until you're dead. But now I've digressed into some kind of whatever it was, that in the end or the beginning, I could know nothing about, or at least choose to ignore most of the time, while now carrying two of the four bottles of wine and our impulse buy of fresh chorizo imported from Mexico. (They wisely keep it in a refrigerator right under your money-counting hands at the cash register.) We both light up despite hitting the steep hill to our place, because regardless of the incline, this is the final stretch.

Anton opens one of the glass-paned double doors of

our large rented house, currently for two, and we enter the big, bright openness of the connected living room, kitchen, and dining room–turned–recording studio, and straight in, it's back into the lab for creation time again for Anton and his assistant.

Working on a song I will come to know later tonight as "Mansions in the Sky," it's what's next on the menu today, and in the time it takes to sip a glass of red down, the rootsy chiming acoustic track and vocal exists, and the song's continuing creation is like a great balled cloud floating in the center of the high-ceilinged room, morphing and expanding further around the room throughout the day as each track is added. He plays back what he has so far, and I wonder how much, if any the words are inspired by once again having sent the entire rest of the band fleeing for the cover of the regular world.

Would you forgive the awful things I've done ...

Then it's time for the tambourine track, which I do sitting in a small chrome with green leather padded fifties diner-style chair on our dining area's black-and-white checkers. It's an unintentional fifties rock 'n' roll rebel set, and I wear the headphones upside down so as not to flatten my mess.

There is no feeling like hearing a new in-progress song during playback when, for the first time, it now has my own presence on it. In this case, my steady stamp-like train never stopping throughout once it starts, yet in time with Brian Jones's borderline beat-dragging tambourine performance on "Time Is on My Side." I love his tambourine on that one, mostly because they left in a few out-of-time beats, hitting home the song's subject matter even further, the sixties message itself of "Do your own thing in your own time," or "march to the beat of your own drum"—or tambourine in this case. Maybe I just read too much into things, my all-time favorite bands, I mean.

By the second verse, I decide the lyrics of this new song are not about those other guys at all. He's not asking forgiveness from anyone, not on this plane of existence, anyway. Then I man the mighty RECORD button as he double-tracks the rhythm guitar with a more low-end rootsy and less bright-sounding one. Just as soon as that's done, we begin another track, and a signature-sounding Anton guitar solo is snake-wrestled down in one, and the song is done, just like that. It's a tune that would have also sat perfectly on *Thank God for Mental Illness*, and as we listen back to the finished song, I appreciate the nostalgic feelings it gives me of those rough-and-tumble San Francisco days.

Some street-style chorizo tacos and more wine, and then Anton goes to the mighty B3 organ in the corner to tinker more with the sound he's planning to use for a song he is going to record with Miranda later. He plays long, extended, vibrating notes, turning the place into a churchlike space, and as the chords shiver long, I am reminded of that day last year in Santa Cruz (a town I have no idea I will be randomly exiling myself to in the not-too-distant future) when we'd bought it with fresh TVT signing dime.

Anton, "Tex," and I were on a road trip up north, collecting vintage gear, and the big vintage instrument score that day was at the Starving Musician music shop on the outskirts of the sleepy surfing town's "action." It's a huge store, as far as the needs of the seemingly predominant college ska punk bands and folky seafood-restaurant-performing scenes here, and Anton finds treasures abound, an original 1960s oyster pearl Ludwig drum kit just like Ringo's, a twelve-string 360 Rickenbacker, and the Hammond B3 organ.

Moving that organ up and into the back of the small rented U-Haul truck was a task, something as you know, I'd done once before, as it's basically a double-tiered church organ with a row of large foot pedals, all housed in lacquered mahogany and quite a large piece of musical furniture. Still, it was impossible not to join in on the excitement of Anton's shopping scores, as this was not a mere spree of pure material shopping. It may have resembled one insofar as the ritual of the retail-ness of the experience, but this was in fact, something so much more.

These were visionaries' tools of magic to be used for creating The Brian Jonestown Massacre's music, vintage instruments that have been passed down through time to different owners and bands like they were living reincarnated lives. Some instruments' individual lives are spent better than others, after one owner providing a life on the big stages, to the next who may choose to keep it under a sheet in a garage, then to perhaps many years on a church pulpit, then to being banged apart by somebody else's kids until broken, then fixed back up and put in a shop for sale to be purchased and used to make BJM albums. Who knows what or why, but where anyone can now hear Anton gave them a good life.

Then there's the other kind of gear shopping, not the new toy kind that is fun, but the boring picks-and-strings kind. I'm tagging along with him to complete the personally dreaded task of picking up said music gear supplies at Guitar Center. This experience is more than quite a few groan levels above the torture sessions of old, back in the San Francisco days when we'd have to go to musician-snobby guitar shops like Haight Ashbury Music or Rocker Guitars, at least to me anyway. This here today is entering into the LA hair metal mothership, Guitar Center's flagship location on Sunset Boulevard.

Anton and I get out of Dutcher's borrowed backup car and slam synchronized front doors that seem to wind-blow the tall palms above, but then I'm probably just stoned and more likely it's the windy gray skies that backdrop them.

His steady stride is filled with lack of reluctance and puts him a few paces in front of me as we round the corner onto Sunset Boulevard proper. I gaze fondly at the El Compadre Mexican restaurant across the street as we approach the entrance area of Guitar Center, where I then hesitate a moment, just to throw up what mental forcefields I can before entering this giant fortress of crap. The blaring cacophony that lies within will be assaulting us from all sides, adding grate to every second we are on the other side of the glass doors.

The store's outer entrance is open and theater-like, with display cases housing historic instruments, while the sidewalk itself leading to the doors has been covered with hundreds of cemented-in handprints, a la Hollywood Boulevard's "Walk of Fame," all pressed into the concrete by some of the most major rock gods. As we begin to walk over them, it almost feels as if the imprinted hands of

Aerosmith, Ted Nugent, Kiss, and many of the other hairy metal hosts are reaching up to grab us by the ankles, as if trying to stop us from entering. Their managers and agents know we carry very different torches, of the kind that can burn all of this rock god shit down to the ground in fact, and if I may, inspire people to do a redo on what rock-and-roll means to the body popular. That's the plan, anyway. As those various handprints try to trip us up, suddenly, other handprints, like those of Keith Moon, Bo Diddley, and Johnny Cash all help slap away their tripping fingers from our feet, and we now walk through the doors unfettered.

Once inside, it's a very sterile place, made over with lots of varnished wood and matte black motifing, as if one could feel they were in a giant recording studio where Sammy Hagar is about to make horrible scrunched "feeling it" faces in the vocal booth, and now Dave Grohl is suddenly supposed to be cool for some reason. Punk rock's inclusion into the rock gear retail mainstream is still somewhat recent, and so the Green Day effect is only just beginning to integrate into these types of *ROCK* places, where whoever from whatever the era, be it Les Paul to Jimi Hendrix, are all filtered through the almighty hair net filter of what it all meant specifically to the eighties hair metal meaning of what it means, and this is the grand temple of all such thought.

In the giant labyrinth of departments, one must first pass straight into the belly of the beast, the electric guitar room, where a literal gazillion guitars hang on the walls in rows from every wall, including roof and ceiling, while the chaotic sounds of separate solo crappy jamming now surrounds. Despite this being a place devoted to music, I feel about as out of place as I would at a fishing gear convention with the dominant eighties hair metal vibes in here, and this place is indeed like a fort's armory to supply all sounds that stink. (Sorry, it's hard to be all Zen all the time about these sorts of things now that the entire Britpop movement itself has seemingly imploded for good.)

For less than ten dollars an hour, Guitar Center employees are forced to engage with customers in order to get a decent wage-defining commission by pushing product, and so by simply entering the room, we are approached by someone pretending to care about what we want. He is young and seems to be new to the job, or at least the retail art of pretending to care in public. I actually feel more at ease with that than I would if it were one of the much more miserable and jaded older types revenging against all for personal success dreams now long dead. This kind of kid is a low-level snob, signified by being defiant yet self-betrayingly skittish. Like he has seen on other people what his persona is supposed to come off like but hasn't been around all this long enough to navigate knowing how it all works. For now, he will just kind of do the uninformed thing in a standoffish, can't-be-bothered way, that also won't leave you alone.

"I just need a capo," Anton delivers like a spaghetti Western antihero asking the local kid which bar the rival bandito gang are drinking at.

"You wanna go to the acoustic guitar section for that," he bemoans with defeated excitement before vanishing within the audio clouds of guitar solos festering everywhere like fart clouds. We head in the direction his half-flopped finger flicked toward and then on down five steps made of metal grating, like this is some sort of industrial zone of rock dude danger, and into the silent acoustic guitar chamber made of all varnished wood interior. Further varnishing is represented throughout, as still guitars hang from everywhere like dead wooden bodies in a folkie butcher shop. This is where we learn the electric guitar section kid doesn't know what he's talking about, because the capos are up by the front registers, where we first came in. This is annoying, but on the other hand, if it had been in here things would have begun to feel a little *too* easy.

Now looking for possible tambourines, we next enter the connected drum chamber, with walls and floor completely covered in drums. Standing in the middle of the showroom floor is another Guitar Center employee with shiny Ronnie James Dio hair, who is twirling drumsticks in his hands. He looks at us in our sixties gear and grins to himself with a shot glass's worth of amusement and a bathroom bump of scorn. Continuing the drumstick spinning, he approaches us, now wearing an evil drum solo grin, like he's all crazy with his hair metal nun chucks or something. Here we go.

Anton turns his back on him and ignores this whole little performance, so I throw up a finger before the snub-job registers with his … whatever it is. "Hey, do you carry tambourines?"

"A tambourine, huh?" he says with half of him still following Anton, who's already picking out the drumsticks he wants. "Okay, check these puppies out." He's now walking backward the way he came while adding some "gimme gimme" finger gestures, just to show his complete command of the situation. On the wall now behind him is a wide and varied selection of screw-mount tambourines made to be used on drum kits.

"Uh, no, I don't mean one you screw on a drum kit. Like handheld."

"*Ohh*, heh, yeah, you mean like a Stevie Nicks tambourine, riight?" This actually isn't a question because he just keeps doing this interaction in his own private drum solo style as he leads me to a column where some packaged and loose tambourines are hanging. "I think we have some of those. Yeah, here."

Suddenly, he's holding a plastic crescent moon–shaped one out toward me in a done-deal, mission-accomplished, what's-next-in-my-life way. I already know I don't want it, but just to finish the mission in an effort to start again, I take the tambourine, which is in a box with a picture of what it is on the front, because why would anyone even want to know how it sounds first? *It's a tambourine.*

"No, sorry, not this kind."

"O-o-o-k … well … here's this other one," he says, this time holding another plastic one. It's round at least, but has a drum head with an image of praying Jesus hands on it.

"I don't like plastic ones, man. I'm looking for a wooden one."

"Ahhh, wood. Wood-wood-wood—dude! Here we go. Wood." By his tone, I am apparently crazy or shy a few *whatevers* and he hands me a tiny wooden toylike tambourine only big enough to have four regular jingles.

He gives it a little shake and smiles the drum solo smile again, like he's suddenly totally ruling everything and can't believe how stoked he is to be doing so. I can only shake my head in disapproval, hence delivering a fail, which in a now plot twist suddenly topples him off of his throne of being the de facto expert on the ins and outs of everything within his chamber. Once again it is verified that I have no business to engage in by being in here, but that's okay. I'll stock up the next time we go to the Mexican marketplace on Olvera Street.

Anton is across the room grinning while shaking his head in that way that makes me wonder if it's my own fault when things like this happen to me, like I am not using some special power we all have that I'm not aware of. He then just shrugs his shoulders as I've now caught up and so we continue on through the keyboards chamber, then DJ gear, and finally into the chamber of studio recording gear. As we do this, there is from every corner of every chamber the rain machine downpour of missed memos in the form of sounds from various solo jamming drums, synth pianos, guitars, and more random spurting and stuttering.

Anton's already got everything we really need for his professional home studio, but he lingers at a long row of display microphones, just to see what's here. "Aww, *yeah*," we suddenly hear from behind. It's another commission-seeking employee. "If you're looking for the latest ribbon mic, you'll never do better than that new R-121 there," he says, picking a box up he thought Anton was checking out.

"This little puppy has a thicker, more resilient ribbon,

and a neodymium rather than alnico magnet. At a distance, the R-121 could be mistaken for a small-diaphragm condenser ..." and all I hear now is the Peanuts classroom teacher meets Jeff Spicoli, which blah-blah-blahs a few more seconds before Anton cuts him off.

"Okay, check this out. I'm using a 1940s RCA 44B that blows this thing away."

Meanwhile, the guy is actually still going through his spiel. "... and the Switchcraft XLR connectoron is recessed precisely in the cylinder's bottom en—*wait.*" It's suddenly registered. A hushed reverence suddenly overcomes him, then he says back almost in a whisper, "An original? The most sought-after, most used, and copied masterpiece of acoustic recording ever made?"

"*Yeah,*" Anton returns, "and I have two of 'em. So, no thanks."

We leave him standing there like a broken robot. As we realize we have to go back through the guitar chamber again to get out of this huge labyrinth, and also because how many times in life do we have to redo life challenges, I ask you, where someone somewhere is jamming Seinfeld slap bass jams but with an angular urgency that doesn't seem to exist anywhere outside of a Guitar Center showroom floor, yet is a sound that is always being played constantly in every store location simultaneously, while from another corner the worst generic-sounding distortion pedal is being put to the Metallica practice amp test, when suddenly one of the much more miserable jaded older types revenging against all for personal success dreams now long dead I'd mentioned earlier is suddenly here to bring the big reveal that this is, in fact, the most dangerous level, the center of the hive.

"Whoa, you guys look like you could need some help," he threatens while pushing up his indoor aviator shades that have curves like his beard's manicured bottom edge. His hair is feather-metal poofed, shirt collar is flipped up on his Guitar Center two-button, quarter-sleeve job. "Let me guess, you guys like the Beatles," he says as he eyes us from head to toe with sarcastic supposed seen-it-all-ness. "*Okay*, here's my good deed for the day. A little education on old vintage gear like Vox guitars. First thing you need to know is …"

Five minutes later, we're walking away toward the cash registers as the younger guitar section employee from when we were in here in the first place sweeps up the older, jaded employee into a dustpan. What bugs me about places like this is that nobody seems to understand that music genres and styles are made to be broken and rebuilt, which is how they all started in the first place. To be stuck in specific regiments of music types and forms strictly adhering to how they do and don't work, to have these stiff rules in making music, is the loss of freeform flexibility with both the past and future, and ultimately these musical belief chains tie one to a specific time and place that will inevitably be left behind with the spinning of the world. Just walk into any Guitar Center. Adapting to fresh thoughts and forward-thinking is not what they are selling, and music is squandered into zombifying age-old trends, where today another smarmy guitar know-it-all gets schooled into dust and the world keeps on spinning. I know there are always exceptions, but after experiences like today, I need to do a little snobbin' of my own.

We finally get the capo from the cashier dude, who somehow has even more attitude than all the other guys put together, as you would, I suppose.

Even the Butler ...

Fear and Lenny

The living room is extra bright with sunny day refracting off the extra-tall white painted walls full up with the chiming sounds of "Whoever You Are," and all is well in the sound department for the next *Strung Out in Heaven* US tour leg. I join the circular formation around the living room, where on my right is our ringleader, Anton, groove-dipping his body down into each intent-filled rhythm strum in his immersed instructional way. Next to him is Adam, and as the newest addition, the main recipient of Anton's animated nature, as he looks back while stealing glances at his chord hand from under a slightly furrowed brow. The situation seems to be drooping his rooster haircut some, but he is determined and will achieve fluff up. Next over and opposite me is Charles, bobbing with his bass and in the groove, with Billy almost hidden behind the kit positioned in front of the double-glass doors. Rounding us out is Jeff, mouth slightly ajar and eyes closed in a sleepy strumming trance.

After rehearsal, everyone else splits. Anton catches a ride with Billy somewhere, and Jeff goes off with Adam, leaving me alone in our latest abode. I lie out on my side and dig an elbow into the living room carpet among the fully set-up gear and start going through the *L.A. Weekly* entertainment section, when suddenly I hear a *knock knock knock* on one of the glass front door panes. There's Lenny, peering though, doing the sideways hand salute/glare visor move. Our sunglasses meet, and I wave him in. Today he's in flowing white wares for some reason, like Anton is most of the time these days. Lenny quickly reveals this was his costume for some car commercial he was an extra in earlier today. He's also wearing a wide, proud smile and ready to impress, but the proposed impressee isn't here. This causes him to deflate some, in that way an actor does right after walking off stage during a scene where they are playing somebody super stoked on something. Now, here we are together in this dual side-stage reality, because honestly I'm not all that jazzed to see the guy, and he didn't drive here from downtown to find just me.

Anyway, now shifting down to second-tier impressing, he perks up slightly while recounting the scene, grinning large again now at the thought of himself in the commercial, where apparently he was like the leader in some kind of nighttime Joshua Tree meditation session of hippies or something. Then a new car flies by like a spaceship, or I don't even care, because now I'm busy pondering if the new film adaptation of Hunter S. Thompson's *Fear and Loathing in Las Vegas* is worth the holy fuck effort of riding the public transportation bus all the way out to Santa Monica. Lenny, meanwhile, is still smugly going on about this and that and the other while his hands orbit around his large, natural auburn afro, which is actually pretty impressive for being totally natural. This plus the fact he comes over almost every day, hoping someone has quit so he can get in the band (eventually he will, but like a year from now, after I've left LA), helps in my decision to go to out the Nuart

138

Theater, despite involving the one-hour-and-forty-five-minute bus trip, because Anton and I don't have our own car. That's bad but also good because both of our surnames are doubled with Trouble, like the hyphen married people get.

Lenny lives in the opposite direction, so I can't catch a lift anywhere along the way, but that's okay, because as you can probably tell, I'm eager to make this a solo act. It's my first escape from the house in several days, but right from the start, there's forty minutes of waiting for a bus that was scheduled to arrive in seven. I get that excited feeling, finally seeing a bus coming down the road; it's not worthy of such a reaction, but after you stand in one place on an intersection as boring as Sunset and Echo Park Avenue while periodically turning your neck to the left every minute or so to see if it's coming, a couple dozen times later, when it finally is, it's like a brightly candled birthday cake being carried toward you from across a room crowded with friends.

While public transportation makes perfect sense for navigating cities like San Francisco or New York, it makes less than zero for navigating through Hollywood because no two things you ever need to do are ever anywhere near each other and each bus line experience is its own forever. Especially when going from somewhere like Echo Park all the fuck way out to Santa Monica and having to stop at every single block the entire route. Apparently, there is a metro rail system expanding to this part of LA, but who knows where I will live by whenever that happens. I walk up the three steps and push change into the meter.

As usual the bus is mostly empty and I take an aisle

seat, then reach out to a discarded *L.A. Times* newspaper across the divide featuring a cover story of Frank Sinatra's funeral. He'd gone up (or down) to reconvene the Rat Pack party with Dean Martin and Sammy Davis Jr. earlier this month. This paper is over a week old, which just goes to show, but as I don't watch TV much or listen to the news on the radio it's a fallen-tree-law situation in that no news is good news, and this printed time capsule made of a felled tree is rendered informative.

Looks like celebs of all make were there, along with a who's-who of who's still alive from those swingin' Vegas scenes of yore, Kirk Douglas, Tony Bennett, Joey Bishop, Angie Dickinson, Nancy and Frank Jr., Don Rickles, Liza Minnelli, Mia Farrow, Wayne Newton, Milton Berle, Tony Curtis, Sophia Loren, Diahann Carroll, Robert Wagner, Debbie Reynolds, Anthony Quinn, Quincy Jones, Dionne Warwick, and so on. Huh. As I bring the two page edges together then pull the next two pages out, I suddenly realize the oddness of first reading this en route to see Hunter S. Thompson's harrowing side of the Las Vegas experience, while the entertainer most synonymous with the hip history of the place has just been laid to rest.

Looks like Europe has just adopted a single currency system, but the UK said *sod that*. Reading this fresh factoid triggers memories of BJM's semi-recent first trip to London, back when Dean and Matt were still around. I fold the paper in half and lightly frisbee it back where it was, then slide over to the window to watch all the whatever fly by.

Back then, on days like these, Matt would be my wanderer-in-arms, and while I won't necessarily miss his often overtly negative outlook while on tour, off the road he was a good egg. Like when during the recording of the *Strung Out in Heaven* album he went out of his way to involve me beyond just percussion in his song "Got My Eye on You," where I could display my enthusiasms for Mick Jagger's "Time Is on My Side" style inter-song rants and Steve Marriott's soulful one-liners of enthusiasms going in and out of song choruses such as "Bombs away!" Or "Now, listen!," those moments when the singer ups the level of conviction and seems to go into a one-on-one, in-your-face conversation with whomever it is in the song that's got them so worked up.

A whole lot later, I enter the small but big single-screen theater having no way of knowing that these days I am living right now will one day be played out on this very same movie screen. *Fear and Loathing in Las Vegas* starring Johnny Depp and directed by Terry Gilliam is pretty great most of the time, but despite the source material, also feels kind of oddly "straight" in sections due to the over-the-top sets and costumes that at times come off more *Labyrinth* than a mind-bending face-melter. Still, it's a major score for anti-establishment drugger freaks that mainstream Hollywood would even allow this to happen, and the actors are amazingly good.

I remember first reading the Hunter S. Thompson book in high school, as you do, then *The Rum Diary*, and later reading his earliest book, *Hell's Angels,* all the way through in a single all-night amphetamine-fueled session. Amphetamines don't really work out in movie theaters though, no matter how much you are enjoying the film. I remember walking down Haight Street one time and seeing that the Beatles *Yellow Submarine* was playing at the Rev Vic. Despite being totally whacked I *had* to go in and see it, but then once in my seat, I wasn't able to sit still and spent the whole movie either doing sit-down seat dancing or pacing behind the back row and going out for a smoke every ten minutes. Sometimes I miss amphetamines, but not enough, and anyway these are different days and there's nothing I even want or can do about that, despite it not even being two years since my rocker withdrew the restraining order.

When the movie's over, I call our Mafia boss lookalike and act-alike new band manager from the payphone across the street, figuring it's better to take him up on the offer I'd turned down from yesterday to accompany him to the nearby Troubadour and get a ride home after, rather than deal with the years it will take to get home on the fuck bus. I guess there is some band playing there that he might manage or whatever, and at least I can imagine what it would have been like back in the day, but unfortunately this is the late-nineties Los Angeles music scene and the band is just what that sounds like.

While all this is going on, I also have to power through another managerial "big plans" BS session, including such far-flung topics as putting together a performance of *Their Satanic Majesties' Second Request* in its entirety as a stage show, with sets and choreography going on around us. ("If Anton doesn't want to, I'll just make him do it," ((*yeah, riight*)) and BJM going back to London already again this year (okay, this second one actually happens). We finally leave, but then halfway

142

home he needs to make a stop at some restaurant on Sunset Boulevard.

He pulls into a small parking lot and then groans while staying covertly expressionless as a valet approaches. We get out as he hesitantly gives him his tip-inducing car keys, and I follow him up a few brick steps and into the candlelit darkness within the white stucco bungalow-style chi-chi restaurant that's not old school or cool in any way but people don't care for some reason. Suddenly we find ourselves holding the door open for Cassandra Peterson, aka Elvira, Mistress of the Dark, which I guess isn't all that weird, as this is Hollywood, and you can expect to see famous people walking around from time to time, but then, in front of us, waiting at the restaurant's host podium, is Pee-Wee Herman. I have just enough time to do a dandruff check on him before he is escorted inside. I turn to remark on the no-apparent-dandruff situation, when suddenly there is Jon Lovitz from eighties *Saturday Night Live* approaching us. He did the "Liar Guy" Tommy Flanagan character, who's actually not all that unlike some of the musician people around LA, when I think about it (Lenny), which I won't until later because it's very bizarre suddenly seeing this comedian shaking hands with my manager; apparently they are friends. Jon Lovitz seems pretty bummed out about something but not quite in the same way I was bummed to see this guy earlier. As we are introduced, he smiles politely but then goes back to somber as he reveals this is his fellow former *Saturday Night Live* cast member Phil Hartman's wake. It was so all over the news this past week that even I couldn't miss that his wife killed him and then herself, which is pretty gruesome. It's all very bizarre being here among what I'm now seeing is a room full of comedic entertainers all grieving together.

The vibe is actually very much Sinatra doing "Send in the Clowns," and so, speaking of fear and loathing, suddenly I remember back in my early twenties watching Phil Hartman play Frank Sinatra comedically hating on Sinead O'Connor after she ripped up a photo of the pope during a recent live music performance on the show. Though musically she wasn't totally my thing, being that this was the Republican-dominated early nineties, I was incredibly impressed by this, a brave act of righteous, ahead-of-her-time defiance, which unfortunately resulted in her career being completely destroyed by the powers that be. Then it came out later that the pope had actually been advancing the careers of priests whom he knew were child molesters.

All popes get to go to heaven regardless though, seemingly, as that's the gig, up there hanging on the big main stage-cloud with Frank, Dino, and sweet Sammy (except being a Jewish convert and brief Satanist, he would probably need a fake ID to get past the pearly-doors man), harmonizing with the big O.G., G-O-D "ol man" himself, who is so laid back and swingin' that apparently he can invent everything ever yet doesn't even care that with a single thought, he could turn his hair from gray back to whatever it was before everything was.

Absolutely Not Necessarily

It was still there. A full, 1.75-liter bottle, just sitting on a fold-out table in an empty dressing room. *It* being a Bombay Sapphire, as in a London dry gin artifact that, in fact, comes from the 1980s Bacardi era, having originated from the 1761 Bombay Dynasty, imbibed with a buzz value that cannot be enthused about properly in sober mind. Its precious jewel-like blue glass bottle design is refracting multiple shafts of light straight into my guzzling eyes, and once in there, they mingle with my twinkle from eyes to toes. I am at once intoxicated with its spell as it weaves within me the prospect of getting intoxicated.

Suddenly, I'm inside the room. I raise the glimmering blue rock handle-bottle, too beautiful for a handle. I do it slowly, like a cat burglar lifting a rare jewel from a museum's glass case, careful not to disturb any laser tripwire alarms that may be installed. Then, I slide the crystalline bottle into my roomy white leather with blue stitch front-end compartment Canada Airline's sixties repro shoulder and handbag combo.

The challenge of now actually walking out of this room with the booze gem is, I mean the right big rub, mate, is the "BUILT TO SPILL" Xerox paper sign scotch-taped on the door.

It's the massive 1998 CMJ Music Marathon Festival and industry conference taking place in various venues of every size all over New York City. Out of the thousand bands playing over the weekend, The Brian Jonestown Massacre have completed our set at this large ballroom-style venue and are done for the night. The venue had then evicted us from the dressing room for the next band, Built to Spill, so that they could do whatever it is they do in dressing rooms that apparently doesn't include drinking the booze that's in it. The whole thing just makes me sick, and then suddenly, the next thirtyish seconds of this night escape my memory completely.

Glug-glug-glug-glug-glug down to the party tent of my tummy, warm and fuzzy, like lying on a bearskin rug in front of the fireplace.

Then fastly down the hall slower than a bowling ball while passing a few other people milling in and out of the other rooms, then just outside the side-of-stage backstage entrance where I'd left Anton and his new girlfriend, Tara, whom he'd met through Ondi recently, which I somehow didn't know about until after the fact. Also with them are our tour manager, Brad, and new guitarist, Adam. Built to Spill are about to hit the stage any minute, to play music that people of this time are excited about. Tara is slight in frame, blonde, and apparently an indie movie actress in films people sort of care about. She seems pretty cool. She'd brought actress-comedian Sandra Bernhard to our last New York show at Coney Island High, and when asked about my stage presence, she responded that I was "brilliant." Word must already be all over showbiz about it.

All of this sussing out of the situation in real time is suddenly disrupted by a very abrupt and seriously alpha circumstance when the Built to Spill singer's first in-between song banter consists of "So, apparently, The Brian Jonestown Massacre stole our bottle of gin from backstage. *Real fucking cool*, have fun with that," he relays, mixing fact with sarcastic well-wishes.

They all turn their heads and look at me simultaneously with wordless *Whaaat?!* smiley faces.

I'm not ready to put my hands above my head yet. "Welll, they weren't even drinking it! It was just sitting there—unopened!" I whisper-exclaim, expecting a group shock response to that last detail.

Then Anton, who with the help of Tara is sober and super together again, has to explain it to me. "Some people request booze for *after* their show, y'know? They don't drink until after they play."

"*Huh?*"

Brad anticipates another dropped beat by chiming in with grin accompaniment, "Boy, one thing is for sure—he doesn't sound too happy up there. You should probably put it back if you ever want to play one of these things again."

"*Huuhhh?*"

I had to sneak it back.

But getting that room back into this bottle would be much harder, as now it was public knowledge that skulldiggery was afoot in the indie music kingdom.

I go professional by pulling my beanie out of my bag, and as I'm already wearing black the rest of the way down to Cuban heel town, I am taking on the cat burglar catwalk dressed to the anti-teetotaler tee for the reverse heist job.

I head backstage again, and once past the wristband

147

fuzz, I move my stealth groove down to *casual with intent*, stepping slowly and with only the outside edges of my feet like a hard day's ninja.

When I arrive back at the dressing room, the door is now shut. I slowly drop to my knees and look under the door. No sneakers. Then suddenly, loud blah-blahs echo from back at the front backstage door as two volume enthusiasts are clomping ever closer from down and around the corridor. I have no idea which room they're heading to, but still, it's either see or be seen out here, so I have no choice but to just fling the BUILT TO SPILL door open and duck in.

As science filtered through my senses has promised, there is indeed no one in here, but that's not the only positive outcome. Apparently, the mini tonic bottles had shown up after my heist job was discovered, yet before the band went on, literally a double dose of double-barrel annoyance for them, I presume.

This inner Sherlock Holmesing brings holm that it's more fun being on the jewel booze thief side of reality, and so without further thought ado, I carefully load four rounds of tonic minis around the gin rocket still in my flight bag. I don't like their music anyway, so fuck 'em.

I crack the door open with three fingers and do a quick double rubberneck. Nobody. The gin already inside me finally chimes in on all this with a quip, "Just own it."

Right. Pulling the egg shaker impulse buy from a drum shop register counter from the front buckle pocket of my flight bag, I place it in the vacant space where creased Zee rainbow pak napkins serve as the crushed velvet jewel display bottom where the gin bottle had been. Call it my "calling card." Then, at medium speed, walking down the hall bouncing like a rubber ball, I head back toward the backstage exit, or backstage entryway, depending on your enthusiasm level for the evening, all the while trying to look like my shoulder isn't caring thirty pounds of glass and liquid, which is also what I have to do when boarding airplanes. In the end, and all in all, it would seem that Built to Spill just wasn't built to spill this giant bottle of gin. *Rimshot!*

The next morning, I wake up on a floor mattress in a room with high ceilings and long, thin double windows displaying a fire escape overlooking a Lower East Side street. The room is sparsely decorated and clean, a wooden dresser, a few small shelves in the corner with some books, an old radiator and a few posters of places and things in favor with the renter of this room, who's currently in Europe or something. Despite my heavyweight division hangover, which one might refer to as raging, despite there being nothing "raging" about such a thing, and in fact is more like a heavy muting dullness like the big lead apron you have to wear at the dentist for X-rays. Waking up in an old school New York apartment like this has me thinking of the *David Holtzman's Diary* documentary. It had amazed me, seeing it for the first time a few years ago while alone on a comedown one early afternoon at Diane Perry's while she'd had to struggle through a downtown temp secretary day tweaker style. It did make sense for a druggy with a straight job, bouncing around from office building to office building before anyone can figure out your behavior is in fact rock-and-roll band scene drug related.

Anyway, what had really got me about the movie was that being a documentary, it was "real." It was the sixties, but rather than a stylized dramatization or based in conceptual realism, it was actually a real life example of sixties life in an accessible, everyday way that surprisingly very much resembled the human condition of what was then almost twenty-five years later.

I get up and immediately regret it, but the situation dictates that I can't throw the fight. I stumble out into the kitchen, where I get a face match to the one recognizable voice that is David Timoner. Now, with enough momentum going, I cut the engine and float into the Formica counter, where I can then lean up against a bulbous fifties type of refrigerator.

David asks if I'll please come along to meet Ondi, Anton, and Tara, so they can finish filming a music video for "Going to Hell." Apparently, the previous day's shooting with Anton busking around the city hadn't gone too well, and today's isn't either, and so now I'm being drafted as a questionably useful hung over motivational tool. From what I gather, apparently they felt Anton was not doing Ondi's vision of what he's supposed to be doing correctly.

By now, as far as I can tell, the film they are doing about us is going to be the type of documentary where the filmmaker does things like choose camera angles that position themselves in front of any mirrors that might happen to be around. It was like that in *David Holzman's Diary*, except that I'd found out more recently that the documentary had been faked. All of it—the characters

150

were all his neighbors and friends, improvising made-up scenarios. His girlfriend was hired; the whole film was a big sham. A card trick.

I'm hung over, man, and it's just as I'm about to say this, David observes, "You look kind of hung over, Joel."

All the gin had been gladly shared away last night, but this now left me with no morning dog hair shavings.

"Oh! I know what will solve it." One of the friendly tenants jumps in. "Here, drink this Emergen-C vitamin packet! It works *miracles*. Your hangover will be *gone*." This person doesn't have any idea what they are talking about, but this will not be revealed until after only two blocks I'm worse for heavy wear and completely exhausted.

The farther we walk, the less accommodating the sidewalks become as the crowds just get thicker with people. Being this hung over, I'm starting to spend as much time sidestepping as forward stepping. I'm looking around too much and soon the streets are so crowded, people are even walking upside down above me and straight up and down in front of me. I close my eyes and walk forward only, which seems to work the best for getting somewhere. Now adjusted to this new every-which-way world, I can't help but start peeking diagonally for a liquor store, but like it matters because I don't have any cash left and ATMs aren't really a big thing yet, but I don't have a bank account anyway. My bank is the Bank of Tour Manager Brad, and I won't be able to give him a withdrawal slip at his hotel bed nightstand teller window until later.

On the plus side, none of the upside-down or up-and-down people go diagonal, and eventually things open up a little. Now there's actual breathing room in between the suits, dogs, and babies being walked, telephone booths, hot dog vendors, which then further extends out to elbow room among all the newsstands, florists, fruit stands protruding from markets, until we cut through a park to actual dancing room, walking past the pigeons in the park and all the old ladies and gentlemen perched and slumped on very long benches.

"Hey, how's it going?" I ask as we approach, but they are too into it.

Anton continues with Ondi, "You are making me want to lay down and die right here."

"Okay! great!" she fires back, exasperated. "Lay down and die, and we'll shoot that. Will that work? I'd just like to get something on film today."

He smiles, and without diverting his gaze from something that isn't any of us, he responds, "Yes."

I jump in. "What if then I come walking down the sidewalk and pick him up, 'Waiting on a Friend' style?"

Ondi sets the shot up, and then as planned, here I come along the street and up to Anton lying flat out on the sidewalk to lend a hand down. Then the final shot of the video is of me and him walking away down the street as I throw an arm over his shoulder. What I couldn't know is, this is the last time I'll ever be in front of the documentary cameras.

Rock Star Wars

A long time ago ... when the first of what turned out to be a great many bad Star Wars *movies came out ...*

I get the good news that my older brother Paul has done the previously unimaginable, and he and his long-term girlfriend have just had a kid. I'm now an uncle. This, after my first-ever for-real-deal hangover while en route to London, in 1998 now six months ago, is another life-post sign that I am slow-cruising out of my twenties and into the other kind of older whatever person. I knew the first action to christen my new uncle status was to buy a present for my brand-new niece, Sonja, which means "wisdom" in its Scandinavian origin.

Meltdown Comics and Collectables on Sunset also sells tons of toys, as I'd seen after once being lured in by its mid-century jet-age sci-fi-style neon store sign while on a return march from the Virgin Megastore. I enter its all-glass front interior and into the large store; my walk turns into a little bop. I don't know why that is. It's a child-adult's candy store in here that will wonka every willy's nilly in all ways nerdly.

The whitewashed walls are covered in explosions of art images on paper in an ephemeral kaleidoscope of printed colors made of stacks of rectangles on racks. Comic books, magazines, graphic novels, books, pamphlets, zines, and framed art line the walls as far as the arm can reach, while the carpets are overgrown with store displays of all things the same. T-shirts and toys gather in a far corner's mix, and that's where I find my first bid at potential "cool uncle" status whilst in the "Ugly Doll" section.

Ugly Dolls are little stuffed animals, cute but also kinda "punk" in their freakiness. I pick one out that looks like a baby blue vampire bat, appropriate for what will be her *Addams Family*-esque existence with her rockabilly-punk mother and self-styled sixties outlaw biker father.

I'm liking how easy this all is as I head up to the registers in an in-and-out fashion that's in true in-and-out style. There's only one other customer over there who's in line, but he isn't actually at the counter, so I have to wait back at an orbiting distance because it's actor and mega-teen heartthrob Leonardo DiCaprio, who's got a gigantic island of *Star Wars* toys piled up past his waist. *Star Wars: The Phantom Menace* had come out earlier this year, and Christmas is next month, so I guess he's buying what looks like thousands of dollars' worth of *Star Wars* toys as gifts. Or else he's *really* into *Star Wars*.

There hadn't been a *Star Wars* movie for sixteen years, and during the weeks running up to its release the local news had been giving daily updates on the growing line of *Star Wars* nerd psychos who were camping in front of Grauman's Chinese Theater. Some camped for six solid weeks out there on sketchy Hollywood Boulevard in order to be among the first to see it, only to go the normal kind of psycho upon leaving the theater because it sucked so bad.

Meanwhile, Leo has seemingly become psycho for

Star Wars toys, and this scene I've just walked up on appears to be a one-sided bartering situation. He's in a wide stance, leaning back and stretching his arms out wide as if to say, "C'mon guys, I'm Leo!" using every part of his body along with a big sly grin, but then, by the exasperated expressions on the faces of the two guys behind the counter, this looks like it's been going on for a little while. I guess he's had to go body bilingual, but regardless, they don't seem to be all that eager to be giving discounts to super-wealthy people like the star of *Titanic*, which two years ago became the highest-grossing film in cinema history.

Then they see me standing off to the side, waiting with my single item purchase in hand and accompanying dollar bills. With looks of instant relief, they both wave me over, now making me feel like the sweetheart of the Comic-Con. One is already reaching for a bag, while the other straightens up in preparedness to tinkle the register keys. This all breaks whatever "Leo-mania"-fueled spell he'd been building up until this moment and they are both emanating appreciation for this disbursement of his attempted retail Jedi mind tricks.

I pass my money over the counter while Leo oddly decides to move up behind me, as if getting in line, I guess. They have to do a little currency arranging to come up with my change so I'm waiting when suddenly I hear the sound of him simultaneously snapping his fingers on both hands, then punching his fist into his palm right behind my head.

Click-punch.

A moment later, *Click-punch.*

Then again now signifying this is a beat, *click-punch.*

"I'm not going to get my star discount on *Star Wars* toys," his fingers click-call, "because of this guy here buying some stupid stuffed animal bat," his fist and palm respond.

Click-punch. Huh, he's actually got pretty good rhythm.

The teen heartthrob celebrity actor with a mountain of *Star Wars* toys is really sending a message to the indie rock musician with the little stuffed animal. *Click-punch.* I play it Zen and just stand my ground while taking his hand-smacking smack talk, then give him a casually paced look back over my shoulder in a panache-infused glance that displays all of my high drama-deflecting prowess.

The register guys see that this has all just escalated into an aloof facial expression vs. hooligan sign language situation and hurriedly hand me my change and shopping bag before someone actually says something about whatever this is.

The bigger picture here, I'm pretty sure, is it may be no coincidence that after my display of enlightened nonviolence that day, he then dropped the spoiled teen heartthrob image and traded in his power of fame to acquire discounted *Star Wars* toys for much more important work as a high-profile celebrity environmentalist.

Now on my way to the post office to send off the Ugly Doll, I suddenly remember that weirdly, he and Miranda Lee Richards are cousins. I wish that I'd remembered this back there. Oh well. Either way, I bet I know what she's getting for Christmas.

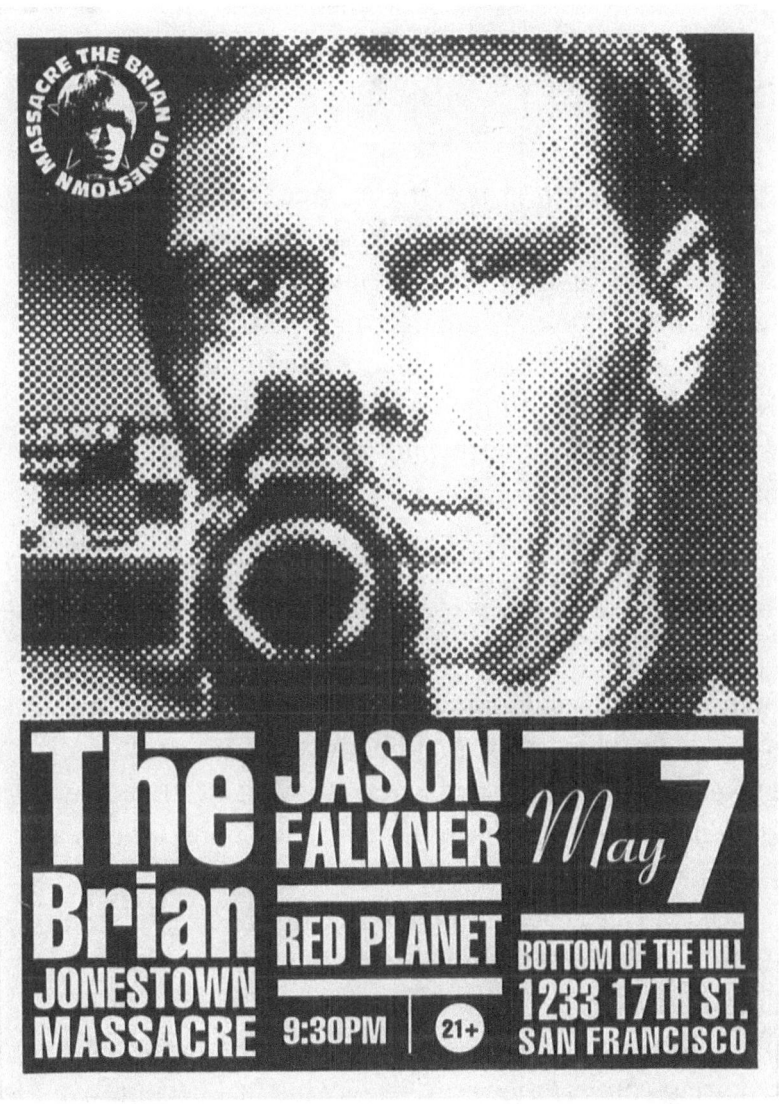

1996 flyer. My concept, Mike Prosenko design

Stinky Fingers

As you remember, or not, if you have drug-induced memory loss issues, then, depending on whether they are short term or long term, equated with how long ago you read the first book, would determine if what I am about to say falls in your particular blacked-out time zone or not. Not too long after all the *Strung Out in Heaven* tours, I wound up making my second big "disappearance" up to Santa Cruz, California.

It was the year 2000, just after the entire world had barely avoided needing to be duct taped back together after the great Y2K disaster, a century-closing event which had also coincided with my being age-86'd out of my roaring twenties and into a depression-era thirties. A few months after I'd left, Anton finally and once and for all kicked heroin, then found a new Los Angeles lineup and started it all over again from the ground floor. Or at least from Frankie's living room couch.

BJM were back doing the live music circuit by the time I finally triggered vibrations down the spiderweb to Los Angeles as to my whereabouts, and Anton immediately tracked me down. Our brief telephone-reuniting conversation was, as in what had become a tradition in this situation, light on heaviness and vice versa, with the point seemingly being, would I want to join them on a full US tour? As mentioned in the first book, this initial reunion run take two doesn't stick. We all know a lot of things don't on the first try, even if, and often because, you want it to more than anything.

The whole tour was already booked, so in just a few weeks, I found myself on the first of two all-day drives, sitting in the back seat of a compact rental car next to longtime BJM understudy now finally officially graduated to third guitar player, Jeff Levitz. At the moment, he's sneering at a pickled peanut perched between two fingers, a stinky five-minute-old roadside regret purchase of Frankie's. Frankie drives as Anton sits in the front passenger seat, tuning us in to Duane Eddy's "Rebel Rouser" on the rental car radio.

Mara Keagle, our "Anemone" chanteuse, was also living in LA and had joined current boyfriend James Ambrose's band, Small Stone, as had other ex-BJM guitar players Jeff Davies and Ricky Maymi, as well as Tommy Deitrick from the old SF band scene, who was now on bass. BJM, for this tour anyway, were just us four riding in the rental, plus we were borrowing Small Stone's rhythm section. BJM manager Michael Dutcher had finally fled the coop, and for this expedition, Mara is the tour guide of not only her band but also what will surely be our drunkard's Romper Room on wheels, a task she is fully equipped for from past time-served dealing with these high levels of volatility that are about to be let out of the starting gate.

I'd flown down to LAX, where James and Mara picked me up in their band van and took me back to their apartment, where I could then be collected by the BJM rental car. She also wanted to make sure I was the one who received the white pages telephone-directory-sized tour book she'd made a second copy of for us, which would at least give us a better chance of making it to our successive venues and hotels. Having a record store job and all, she had deemed me the most responsible one of the BJM bunch.

Unfortunately, we all discover the hard way that I've "still got it" when I promptly forget the tour book at Mara and James's apartment. I don't even realize that I haven't actually got it until three hours down the freeway en route to the first show, which for some reason isn't until Austin, Texas. This was pretty dumb of me, but on some very far-off-in-the-distance, barely audible positive note, it also meant I hadn't yet changed into something else, something too responsible, and so it's also weirdly relieving. Also, Anton and Frankie don't seem to care, as we all recognize the tour book as an itemized catalogue of all that might go wrong for us. We are now free of MapQuest drive times, load-in schedules, and could now proceed with the freedom of never needing to make it anywhere until ten minutes to stage time. I go from the "responsible one" to the in-house go-to "blame for any and all future fuck-ups to the daily schedule for the next three weeks."

I didn't know Frankie, but Jeff Levitz I did know; he used to hang out all the time at our *Strung Out in Heaven* house in Los Angeles during the dark days. He holds up another pickled peanut while the first one continues to slither around in his mouth, to his disapproval, which is enough of a review for me, not that I had any intention of eating one of the disgusting-looking things anyway.

The 2001 tour-initiating doomsday plan was to drive straight to Austin in one twenty-four-hour go. No hotels, crash pads, or otherwise. The blow-by-blow of the incredibly tedious and extremely uncomfortable expedition could only be attempted with the tried-and-true failsafe that is getting totally fucked up.

Like suds in the beaker glass goes a case of beer, but Jeff doesn't drink, which is the good part about him getting us pulled over for speeding. It's night now, so luckily the cop doesn't see the Pabst Blue Ribbon box full of twenty-four "open container" charges between my legs in the front seat.

I keep my knees pushed together, trying to keep the box of empties in the shadows while still finessing a "casual hang" style of a three-inch non-fey-looking kneecap distance. Now nearing the Texas border, it's a minor miracle that all we get is a speeding ticket before the cop somewhat hesitantly drives off. The case of empties goes right there in the desert shoulder ditch, and we all get out and pee while watching his taillights disappear into the distant darkness. Then Anton gets in the driver's seat, putting the rest of us in a flash game of musical bucket seats. As we pull back onto the road, Anton calls "strike one" for Jeff, who has technically just put the tour financially in the red. With no more beer, nor any desire to drink anymore in the car tonight, tomorrow is another today, and so I curl up into fetal and pass out in the back.

Things in this new BJM already feel a bit off, but not in the good ol' off ways; this is a newer shade I'm not familiar with. Anton and Frankie have a sort of roving marauders vibe about them and are clearly a duo on a mission. Despite my valid reasons, technically, I was the one to abandon the ship, and so I wasn't expecting it to suddenly be "just like the old days." We'd changed as you do, rolling with what moving on does to you, and ultimately I'm happy to be asked along. I don't mean to say I feel unwelcome in any way, and despite my borderline uneasy feeling, one thing is for sure—the songs are still great.

"Hey, did you see this?" Raul had asked, interrupting a long record store shift space-out session. Raul is one of my Streetlight friends. Usually in moments like these, he'd be showing me a world psych jazz reissue or sixties French pop compilation I hadn't seen before, but today he's holding up an advance promo copy of a new Brian Jonestown Massacre CD EP that some industry connected person had just sold over the used buy counter. It's called *Zero* and is the first BJM release since I'd split. It's also the first BJM music that I'd have to pay for, which is a weird feeling, but made 20 percent less so after my employee discount.

The songs on this one have a next-levelness to them and sound fresher and more artistically driven to me than most songs on the *Strung Out in Heaven* album. Perhaps with that same special sheen *Satanic Majesties Second Request* has for me, as it was recorded during my OD (original disappearance). Traditionally, he'd always done his deepest work when life had him up against the ropes. I listen to it twice in a row on my way home that night, and I continue to like it more with each listen.

Then not long after, while waking to work with morning BJM ritual jams on, I spot an ambulance parked up right on the sidewalk on the next block ahead. I approach, and as feared, it's the house of the Streetlight Records manager who'd hired me and, in effect, saved my pork chops. He had died of a heroin overdose. I had to take this tragic news to the store, gather the staff around, and announce that the guy we all loved had just died this morning. It felt like the tragedy of heroin was following me everywhere, and this horrific event also brought to light that it was time to make contact down south to LA. I called Randy to get an update. Word was from down there that Anton had finally gotten clean, and word from up here was now somebody knew and could finally tell Anton where I was, replete with phone number.

Morale is getting low in that way it does on the second straight day of nonstop desert voyaging. At least for me anyway, but being that it's about a hundred degrees out and we've been in sitting position for so long now it's like we're taking a victory lap on a flight to Australia, I'm pretty sure I speak for all four of us. By now Jeff Levitz has already become this tour's designated driver as well as grievance sponge, as those two things often go together.

I've only just woken up (again) a few minutes ago, due to the on-again off-again back-and-forth of Anton's driving style complaints versus Jeff's aloof brush-offs. Then Jeff takes these attacks on his driving skills to the stage and begins to verge through the other three currently desolate early-morning empty lanes while going "wheee!", as to add a little more zaniness to this joke he now has going of driving us all off the freeway at ninety-five miles an hour to our deaths.

He turns his head sideways toward me with an expression like I've got to be loving this over here, but Anton's a pretty tough crowd today and immediately proceeds to reach around both sides of his headrest and starts strangling him from behind. "I will *not* be held captive!" he shouts as he shakes Jeff by the neck, who now has stiffened all the way up, white-knuckling the wheel. It's the only way to steady his body, which is a real brotherly way to go about it, rather than grabbing Anton's hands wrapped around his neck and trying to pry them off and letting us all career off the freeway at ninety-five miles an hour.

There goes strike two, which doesn't need to be called because we all just saw it and then some, and all return to just the normal physically uncomfortable. Nobody talks for a while. I can't help but look around for potential strike threes, like we're driving through a desert infested with killer strikes. I'm also fully awake plus tax now and anxious to meet back up with the others. Although Mara's probably going to kill me for forgetting the fat tour book she'd made for us. Mostly I'm excited to play with BJM again, which hasn't been for so long now, not since the end of the *Strung Out in Heaven* tour.

That night in Austin, Emo's is packed, and the music shines. It was like nothing had changed yet everything had changed all at the same time. Either way, I was flooded with what it's all about, the glorious and infinite whatever it is, and the magic box had been opened back up for me and reawakened the feelings that once made up my everyday resting state's face. In this rekindling of the flame, nobody needs to remind me ever again that every good moment passes, and I try to hold on to this feeling as long as I can while it slowly fades away, like an intensely pleasurable high. When you break it all down and put it in order, the biggest picture here is not about the quality of the situations, or in most cases even the relationships. It's that ninety-minute high.

Unfortunately, the budget on this tour is sans TVT cush dollars, and so we can only afford one room for four people with only two beds. Sharing flop style like this was fine back in the Matt, Dean, and Anton days, I guess, but we were all close and I didn't know these newer guys very well. Regardless of suck-it-ups and so-whats, the problem that arises on that first night—and what will from here on out be the permanent hotel room sleeping configuration for the rest of the tour—is that I will be sharing a bed with Jeff Levitz.

Every night it's the same thing. I lie on our shared bed, atop the covers facing Frankie and Anton on the other side of the nightstand, always on the bed by the window. Like me, Anton and Frankie lie on their sides, facing away from each other. Jeff, on the other hand, sleeps flat on his back, in his thick peacoat like a dead soldier waiting to be carried away, while I lie on the stretcher alongside him. Wait, I forgot to turn the sound up; he's also snoring. He's always snoring, and I don't mean just snore-snore; I mean he somehow snores three different ways all at once.

This snoring of three different ways is constant and

all night, like his head is its own all-in-one trio of nasal noises. First there is the classic snore … snore …; meanwhile, his left nostril is doing this wheezing thing, like a cold wind blowing through a dark cave—wheeeee … wheee-eh… But perhaps the most disturbing of all was the right nostril siphoning some of the main snore flow to create its own kind of snore, where no snore was built to go, causing a release of pressure in convulsive bursts, ThhhnNAH! ThhhnNAH!

I just can't help but turn over and stare.

Mwah! Mwah!

Oh yeah, I forgot to mention there's also a facial tic that periodically happens, accompanied by a shiver and jerk that goes Mwah! Mwah!

And a-one, and a-two …

Snore … Snore … Wheeeee … Wheee-eh … ThhnNAH! ThhnNAH!

Mwah! Mwah!

Snore … Snore … Wheeeee … Wheee-eh … ThhnNAH! ThhnNAH!

Mwah! Mwah!

Snore … Snore … Wheeeee … Wheee-eh … ThhnNAH! ThhnNAH!

After staring at the ceiling for I don't know how many years, I turn and look over at a sleeping Frankie facing me from the other bed, a serine smile and half a Prince Valiant across his face. I get the impression that even in his sleep, he finds all of this very amusing.

Mwah! Mwah!

We continue on familiar roads to a lot of the same places played before, some from the first small tour and others from the subsequent larger ones, but either way, it's a relief to be reminded on a daily basis that the up-and-comers had not already become down-and-go-ers, as the mighty glug-glug-glug train keeps a-gluggin' on down the tracks to the next destination on the map.

We hit the big cheesesteak capital of the world that is Philadelphia, and it's either a really good gig or a really bad one, as those seem to be the only two possibilities. Either way, Frankie is excited to party after the show with friends who live here, and he and I drive to an apartment to party down. Now, I've said it before and I'll say it again, because that's what happens when the subject is cocaine, but I'm not crazy about the stuff. In fact, most drugs no longer moved me in the ways they had before. Even my former spirit-chemical-life and code formula, speed, now rendered far too long a security guard night shift of being conscious inside my own brain cell.

But (which is the gateway word to talking about all the drugs that get done anyway), they are chopping new lines every half hour, and every single time, out comes the offer again, accompanied by hopeful looks, until finally I have drunk enough beer to say, "Yeah, fuck it. Gimme one."

And so it goes, line by line we burn the night down to day from kitchen barstools. After a long while, the sun has been out long enough to start looking bored, and even good coke isn't good when it's gone, so I inquire, "Hey, somehow it's nine thirty. Think I could crash on the couch for a few?" I haven't even seen any of the apartment other than this kitchen and the bathroom because those are the first rooms you run into when you walk into the place.

"Sure, man, but Frankie, didn't you say you guys were supposed to be somewhere this morning?"

Frankie jerks into a flash-attention seizure that ends with him perfectly erect and frozen in his stool.

"Wait! What? It's nine thirty! Fuck! You can't sleep! We're gonna be late!"

"Late? Late for what?" I ask, but by his sudden stress level, I'm not really wanting to know in any way whatsoever.

"Anton's at the TVT Records office! We're supposed to be there at eleven!"

"TVT? He's already there?"

"Yes," he states, now somewhat composed. "He went to New York straight after the show last night."

"*Oh.*" I'd just assumed he'd gone to some other spot in town, and we'd all be eventually getting back together today and driving over to New York together for sound check time, which is what we normally would have done in this situation.

"Well, I'm glad we're going to New York already," I lie, "but I don't want to go to TVT."

"Huh, *riight*— you're the one that *has* to go!"

An hour and a half later, we're barreling through Manhattan, and despite being on a tightly packed narrow side street of the Noho District, Frankie is absolutely *flying*. Although this factor is somehow not as harrowing as it should be because Frankie is turning out to be like the Steve McQueen of shoegaze. He'd been a pro competition BMX bike racer as a little kid and then motor scooters, and from there motorcycles quickly followed. He's been driving cars longer than most of us and is of gearhead grade.

Some radio program about Mao Tse Tung is on, I guess because not even the power of music can spruce up the desperate hangover vibe in here as we frantically race to the TVT offices for some reason. It's a *French Connection*–style car chase, except we only seem to be chasing ourselves. The fact that we're not bending fenders and sending mirrors flying in all directions is a testament to Frankie's hotdog driving skills under the pressure of influences. I see the famed Other Music record shop storefront, which signifies we are there.

I wish I could just go record shopping, but as it turns out, TVT and BJM are mutually nullifying the record contract today. Thoughts of the circumstances as to why I was last here at the TVT offices now flood my mind and take me back to the morning of the flight home, after being the first to sign the BJM record deal now almost three years ago and what was then currently the arson site of my mind as I crawled through the burning embers of charred soul back into consciousness.

I unload what's left of the shooter bottles out of my room's minibar at the Soho Grand Hotel and rake up the residue of the fat Andy Warhol's factory-style speed bag I'd been scored by the label into a final finishing line before the Town Car will arrive in twenty minutes. The cocktail mix of memories representing my week in New York are right now a twenty-one-vapor salute as to what a great time was had while being wined and dined on label dime for a days-long celebration of the contract signing. An envelope accompanies the customary morning newspaper sticking in halfway under the door. This paper will be the top floor of my unread *USA Today* tower, while the envelope turns out to be a copy of the week's bill for the room, minbar, downstairs bar, and room service and … *lordy!* I quickly divert my eyes away from its satanic hieroglyphic symbols.

As soon as I leave my room and enter the polished grimness that is outside-world reality, I instantly find myself holding the end of a tail that has just been shed from its weeklong party lizard's body. Now driven out of my disheveled den, the clean luxury of even the hallway feels like a Hollywood set façade, and suddenly I can't tell if the surrealistic dream is the one I am leaving or the one I am entering. What I feel for sure is that this is now the pumpkin hour, and all the repercussions of being outside at this time come crashing in at once.

Would no one put this all on paper to spell out to me how impossible the whole plot was? Only the cleaning maids I pass down the halls really seem to know the truth in their caregiver-like dutiful smiles, also the uniformed lobby attendant who gives me the detention officer eye, then the girl at the check-out desk with the concerned yet amused Nurse Ratched nod. The front doorman's brow slightly furrows at my overly excited thank-you. They all knew this whole thing wouldn't stick. That there'd been some kind of mix-up at the universe's main office, but they weren't telling. They all just smile at me with an assuring "*suuure* …" as I continue my uninformed walk of shame back home.

I pull out one of my booze shooters and open the door to my waiting Town Car with elbow and chin in group salute to the skyscrapers that surround. I get in and pull out another shooter, then fumble through my bag for the ANTON NEWCOMB (signature is missing the last "e") fake identity card our manager had made me last-minute, and I have it, which is good, but unlike the janky yet brand-new condition it was in on the way here, after a week of traveling through the wasted lands of New York nights, it's looking like it's got a bigger hangover than I do, crumpled, frayed, and peeling around the edges. There's even white powder residue caked within the splitting seams, actually quite a bit, so I excavate as much as I can, chiseling it all out and into a pile atop my box-pack menthols lap table. Soon the airport is in sight, and I pull another shooter.

I guess the sight and smell of me isn't ideal for this scenario, and the woman at the check-in counter isn't so pleased to see me. Although my carry-on doesn't include attitude, our brief exchange ends with an angry and sarcastic, *"Why don't you just go have another drink, sir?"*

If you clean off the sarcasm, then this is technically an instruction from an airline representative, so I follow this preflight procedure, which then brings on the blurs for my return. I guess I made it onto the plane because I wake up in Los Angeles five hours later. It's hard to explain, but these moments are the equivalent of an end-zone dance when you're a several-day bender-wasted musician who must figure out the impossible, which is catching a flight solo while under such influences and conditions. The main thing here is that I had crossed the finish line for the team, successfully completed the mission, and nothing could change tha—

CLICK

Frankie turns the car off, and we are now parallel parked across the street from the TVT offices.

I'd already internally decided by the Holland Tunnel that I wasn't going up there. I'd played along with everyone's preferred reality from the very beginning, waived my rights, now that it's all this they can figure out whatever it is now without me.

"I ain't going up there."

"You'rre *not coming up?*"

"Nope."

"Uhh … oo-k, *soo* … you're really not coming up?"

"I'm *not* going up there."

"All *riight*, guess I'll go up and see what's going on."

Everyone on the TVT staff had been so cool, and there was nary a flippant attitude toward us among them. They seemed across the board to be excited about us, and for us to *be* us, in both music and in image, regardless of the popular trends of the times. We were to be a new time fueled by the past to make a better present, "Yesterday and Tomorrow Today." I'd been the one sent here to convince them that we had it together enough, despite everything going on around me at home already suggesting otherwise. I stare across the street at Other Music, the record store our PR person, Adam Shore, had taken me to for a post-signing shopping spree. Examining the window displays takes my mind off of it all, and I start to drift …

Suddenly, Frankie opens the driver's door. "Well, shit man, now I guess they say they can just do what they need to do without you coming up there after all. But hey, Nadine really wants you to come up and say hi."

I turn my head and look at him leaning in the doorway. "Man, I love Nadine, but I'm not going up there." I rest my temple back on my fist and turn to stone so he can see how impossible it would be now that I'm a statue.

"All-*riight*," he returns in an animated last-chance-for-no-regrets fashion, but I'm not falling for it. The door slams, and with it most of the volume from the outside world.

When I was five, way before I got into pounding booze or snorting drugs, I was really into things like hot dogs and ice cream. So, when my mom pulled us off of Meridian Avenue and into the huge parking lot of the Hacienda Gardens Shopping Center for the umpteenth time so far in my sweet, short life, I'm thinking my usual Woolworth's soft-serve ice cream while we shop, or a deli counter hot dog at the ginormous all-glass-front Safeway supermarket. Oddly, we continue on past them both and are now heading towards the very far-end corner of the shopping center, where small businesses taper down into the cross street–border which then suburbia resumes, where feathered birds perch and tweet overhead from playing children with feathered hair.

My mother, who women on TV like Cindy Williams and Linda Ronstadt remind me of (except with our shared facial features), pulls us into one of the all-empty parking spots right in front of a business that I don't know says Hacienda Barbers. "Come on, Joel," she instructs in her intentfully dazed way that does not invite questions as to whatever this is about to be.

Up until now, it was she who had always trimmed my

hair as needed, a few snips along the bangs, a few snips over the ears, except when it accidentally got too long. Then I'd find myself in a carved wooden dinner chair while she, the oldest of five siblings, and her sister, the youngest, my aunt Linda, reduced their past teenage high school beehive science down to the simple little boy's Beatles cut. I would sit there in silence while they strategized, enjoying the full attention it brought me, even though they were looking through me like I was a bonsai tree or something.

The problem this time was that my hair had gotten the longest it had ever been, to a length she felt was beyond both of their combined skills. I'd have to go into the hands of a professional.

All I'd been able to tell so far was that my mom had her game face on, so it was hard to get a read as to how bad this was going to be, like seeing a doctor or a dentist. What was for sure was that she wasn't in the mood to converse, or in other words give any clues away until it was too late. Well, at least there's got to be ice cream or a hot dog on the other side of this.

The barber is an old older man, with impeccably groomed, slicked silver hair and *very* clean. His white uniform shirt buttons up over the right side of his body, like it was bought at a tailor for mad scientists. It gave him a similar look to both the doctor and dentist, who were my two biggest friendly enemies on earth, with their stainless-steel sharp things. I had a sense that things couldn't be quite as bad as that because a salon has a much less captive vibe than an office. Another thing that made this one feel different was his overbearing scent, like when I smell my mother's perfume bottles. Despite his cleanliness and musky-sweet aromas, I still knew he was one of the dislike club.

He puts a stepstool down so I can climb up onto the huge oxblood leather barber's chair. I push back until enveloped in its cover, and it's slightly slick and cold under my legs. He pumps a type of lever, and I rise up in pushes like it's a Willy Wonka contraption. He then wraps a piece of tissue-like paper around my neck tightly, like a paper turtleneck, but too tightly, and now I think I'm not going to enjoy whatever is about to happen.

The chair spins around and away from my uneasy reflection in the wall of mirrors, but then there it is again on the opposite wall. Then the stainless steel comes out. Long, thin, pointed and razor sharp. His scissors are much more serious looking than my mother's bulbous sewing scissors that lived atop a puffy rainbow cloud of yarn balls, and now I know for sure that this can't be good.

He keeps my head pushed down as I watch the little tufts of my hair float down like fat snowflakes. I'd never actually seen so much of my detached hair like this, now all over the checkered floor around me. Although it didn't hurt, it was like he was chopping off pieces of me, the way he did it. Every time, snip, snip, snip, then while he combs, the scissors hover around my face, an inch away from my eye, then quickly darting into action again, like one of Rikki Tiki Tavi's enemy snakes attacking the hair on my head. *Snip, snip, snip.*

It's becoming pretty clear he's going for short, and this all seems like a pretty big deal to me right now, and so while still keeping my head down for the barber, I look up to my mom for help, but the stern look she returns to me is, "Just sit there and don't embarrass me."

Tap-tap.

I lift my head from my hand. It's Frankie. I roll down my window. "Here. They said they were still going to be a while, so I went to that cart on the corner and got you this." He hands me a hot dog.

Better Living Through Other People's Chemistry

Once bread-fortified enough to brave the tech-risen rents back to my sacred beatnik hippie homelands of San Francisco, *Dig!* happened, and as such, fantasy reality becomes reality movie fantasy for real by the time Ondi and David come to San Francisco to record some of us for a *Dig!* DVD audio commentary track.

Anton decidedly hates the way the film turned out, and even if he didn't, he lives in New York now, so for team BJM, it's just Bay Area locals Miranda Lee Richards, Matt Hollywood, Dean Taylor, Dave D, and me all arriving separately but together, which is often pretty much the same as arriving together but separately when it comes to musicians.

Waiting for us is a shit-ton of beer, which apparently is payment for our participation, like we're still a bunch of borderline bum dropouts or something but then it turns out that that's exactly what some of us are as we sign away on a fresh batch of waivers, and Matt and I then proceed to pound down smack-talk mood lube. Dean is looking healthy and happy; his hair is shorter than I've ever seen it and he essentially dresses the same, minus some of the band guy flair. Dave D keeps a friendly but what will always be a customary distance from the three of us because of what happened at CBGB's and our allowing him to be fired by Anton without putting up a fight for him. Miranda is a welcome addition of female energy, whose presence here will double as keeping Matt and Dean's occasional Beavis and Butthead tendencies in check during the commentary.

Despite after winning the Sundance Film Festival's Grand Jury Prize and all the various film festival appearances since, making this my umpteenth viewing of the film, it manages to be fresh, mostly due to finally seeing it with fellow war heroes. We rightfully bond over all the misshapen moves we'd made as they roll out in front of us on the TV monitor. It's kind of fun, but by the end of it I'm "over-intoxicated," or totally fucking wasted, as we say in the indie-drunkard trade. That's when a body full of booze wearing record store employee–grade smarty-pants does what will wind up being called the "Making of the Audio Commentary," or more accurately, "Joel talks a bunch of shit about Courtney Taylor," a name that has recently grown to Taylor-Taylor for some reason. All of this is filmed and unbeknownst to me, will become its own bonus feature on the double-disc special edition. Kids, when you sign a waiver, watch your behavior around those you've waived all your rights to, because "anytime later" is a long time.

I make fun of the Dandy's career-making phone commercial hit song's lyrics, then call him out on other stuff in the movie. I mean, did I really have to put all of that out there? Even if it was true? No. So, that was fucked, and now I'd said what I really felt, musically speaking, which is usually the best thing to do, but occasionally, it's also the worst, like now, when all it can do is cause trouble. However, there it is now, smeared in full over the "forever camera," the camera I'd so successfully navigated not doing anything I would honestly be embarrassed by during the documentary filming. Now, here was this fucked-up fuck-up for all to see and hear for as long as DVDs are the way people watch movies. So, basically forever.

This little item will ironically create the most real "war" between any of the band members yet, despite being so after the fact, a war created by what one could wager had been a semi-fictional waged war. Now, for the first time, there are real threats of physical violence, with Courtney making sure to get word down to me from Portland that he has vowed to kick my butt, and word is, he had even started taking a martial arts class to do so.

I've actually had my own experiences with learning martial arts, but that was way back when I was ten years old, now twenty-five years ago. Like millions of other American kids, the discovery of Bruce Lee had a profound effect on both me and my older brother, Paul. I'd been too young and just missed Bruce Lee's original worldwide popularity explosion, but living within the San Francisco Bay Area, we grew up with all Bruce Lee's movies from a very young age, as he was born in San Francisco and hence a local hero. All five of his films were rebroadcast on local TV station KTVU a few times every year. Then later, when video rental stores became a thing, we would rent them over and over again.

In lieu of a school that taught Bruce Lee's Jeet Kune Do style in our area, Paul found us a Tae Kwon Do class, and we enthusiastically signed up. The class was made up

179

of about fifteen students representing the California race melting pot, with ages running from about eighteen down to me, ten years old. The school was run by a soft-spoken Asian Indian American, and rather than being a strictly competition fighting or self-defense style class, his teachings were from a more Zen approach. I learned about stretching and meditation, an almost impossible task for a ten-year-old who showed up ready for action but instead was first being instructed to be as still as possible. Despite this, I always took my meditation attempts seriously and tried my best to tune out while tuned in to all the new sensations like strong incense and shrine decor.

Our teacher drew heavily from Bruce Lee's philosophies, which had really hooked us in even deeper, and unlike karate, with its predetermined forms and specific order of moves, we were taught a style of Tae Kwon Do that was infused with Bruce Lee's Jeet Kune Do style, but unfortunately, about six months later, our teacher moved out of town and this turned out to be the end of my serious martial arts journey. However, I would take the concepts of flowing movement through honest expression that I had learned through martial arts with me for the rest of my life, including onto the stage. But would my now-ancient skills still work in battle against Courtney Taylor-Taylor of The Dandy Warhols? Despite his lanky frame, it was not without some definition. I've also seen more than one band photo with him wearing a Gold's Gym T-shirt. Was there something to that? All I knew for sure was that I'd better sport my vintage Persol Ratti 23/91 Bruce Lee–style sunglasses.

Someone who could certainly kick my butt with

180

martial arts is Zoe Bell, a fellow documentary subject appearing at this year's Independent Film Festival of Boston. She's the main focus of the film *Double Dare*, which is about stunt women in Hollywood. A blonde New Zealander, Zoe was recently Uma Thurman's stunt double in both of the *Kill Bill* movies, which had a lot of crazy-ass stunts.

As the in-person "subjects" of this year's festival, we are an exclusive club of two, and we seal our status pact by killing a bottle of whiskey while under the supervision of festival curators. We're both on the doc fest circuit, crisscrossing to independent movie festivals around the country. These are the glory days of documentary film, where almost every Friday there is a new one opening at the art house theaters and competing for ticket sales with all the indies and world cinema.

Our whiskey faces slowly smooth out with each shot, and we proceed to laugh a lot over the next couple of hours. She jokingly agrees to be my stunt double once my impending Hollywood career blows up with the success of *Dig!*, and now that I may have a new stunt double, I decide I'm not taking more martial arts classes just for Courtney Taylor-Taylor of The Dandy Warhols' sake.

* * * *

My cab from the Austin airport pulls up in front of the Marriott Hotel. "Can I get a receipt, please?" I ask the cabbie. Transportation is on the short list of expenses to be paid by Island Records' film division, Palm Pictures, the distribution company responsible for releasing the two-disc special edition of *Dig!* releasing on DVD this week. It's yet another documentary-related appearance for me, this time here at the 2005 South by Southwest music festival, to DJ what sounds like a big party for the huge *Spin Magazine*.

He scribbles some and *zzrrrpp*s the receipt away from his thick pad, and I'm very entertained to see that above the pencil filled-in detail lines is what is mostly a *Dig!* ad of my face, apparently having now graduated from milk carton to company write-off receipt poster-boy status.

The next morning, I walk the short distance toward deeper downtown music town, where there are 250 copies of the DVD waiting for me to sign. I'm doing a hangover solo today, despite not having met anyone last night, a situation that tends to make me communicate with my bottle tops more. I kick a rock and watch the brown vapor trail of dust it makes in the soft dirt. Then as I get thicker in the chili, I can hear loud rock coming from various sides of the next intersection, and after walking through a few blocks of more, I'm there.

Robert the Palm rep is the naturally tussled yet plain unshaven type one might expect working for an art house/foreign cinema/music/documentary film distribution company. He starts our relationship off the way I have found to be one of my favorites, with a "want something to drink?" Within moments, I am presented with my glass of motivation before unveiling the five boxes of special edition DVDs I have come here to sign as industry promo giveaways. Luckily, there is a small balcony for me to sit second-story style while overlooking groups of smiling sun dresses, concert T-shirts and city cowboy hats walking to and thither and from and fro, bros and girls all on their way to various daytime gigs going on all around.

Being up here reminds me of Matt Hollywood and I watching Iggy Pop from the Drixol Hotel balcony back during the first time I'd ever been to SXSW, or Texas for that matter, despite almost never making it this far after the aftermath, or, after Matt kicked me in the head. I touch the small permanent scar on my temple.

I eventually punch the clock and we move it over to the big outdoor stage at Stubbs, where some old ladies are doing a New York Dolls tribute. But then Robert informs me that it's actually the real New York Dolls, who are apparently the latest band to have gotten back together to make a record that stinks so they then have an excuse to tour under the flag of relevancy and play the old songs everybody loves. Once singer David Johansson has another on-stage hit of his St. John's wort, "Personality Crisis" kicks ass, and the huge crowd celebrates the not-*so*-long-ago heyday of communal music subculture lifestyles.

The next morning, I get another MySpace message from someone on behalf of Dave Navarro from Jane's Addiction, who's wanting me to play in his all-star cover band Camp Freddy, which is like a Guns N' Roses, Stone Temple Pilots, Jane's Addiction supergroup, and yet despite no longer being in BJM or the rich rock star paycheck that this gig would bring, this is not the answer to the musical question.

The other unanswered question of the morning is why the *Spin Magazine* party starts soon, which upon my 11 a.m. arrival is quickly revealed to pretty much just be an industry schmooze-fest in a rented house. James Iha from Smashing Pumpkins has been slated to DJ this event with me, if that is the right word, and he is a long way from the *David Letterman Show* or wherever he's normally supposed to be. It's virtually effortless for us to form a mutual indifference society together, as he plays ironic rock junk and I'm wasting hard-won Turkish psych, French yé-yé, Japanese surf, and Italian mod-lounge vinyl. *Dig!* seems to be nowhere on the radar here, other than a poster-sized version of the cab receipt.

Now resigned to boredom, I sit and melt along with the ice in my drink when suddenly, the front door kicks open and through the blasting sunlight emerges Anton and his new BJM #2 and sidekick and physically younger brother candidate, Frankie. I blink away the blindness and they come into focus, with what I can only describe as shit-eating grins on their faces. It's like they were here to cause trouble, which is exactly what this place is in need of right now, and after some new-sheriff-in-town hellos, I sit back and watch, grateful to see some real as Anton musses up the party's hair some, working the patio crowd in random small-group conversation enlightenment invasions. As welcome as this is, I'm also partially on edge, as I haven't seen him in person since before Sundance and the movie release.

Anton quickly gets bored, as you would at any bunk party and especially one that is supposed to be exclusive and hence *cool*, and his bemusement implies it's somehow my "fail" or something. I wonder what they are even doing here in Austin at all. They aren't playing, but maybe they are doing something with his friends the

Raveonettes or who knows. I could ask, but reasons are often not things in situations like these.

He probably only came to this party to call me out for continuing to support the film, I reckon, but then we hang out some and it appears that he is and he isn't, but either way very much doesn't seem to give a shit anymore and is, in fact, exuding a peaceful, unspoken bemusement to it all. This, however, will prove to be a hard state to maintain now that it's all about to go nuclear with the release of the DVD. Regardless, he's already said his war-and-peace to the press months ago, and now we are just three very buzzed ones, sitting here this midday and I've finally got a breeze of relief blowing in that I guess he's not mad at me.

It makes me wonder how things might have gone had the cameras been around for his first arrival in San Francisco and the earliest, most focused days. The laser beam surgical accuracy days, *the beginning of everything days. That* is what was always supposed to have been his movie, but as it was, they really caught him at his lowest point. Or he caught them at it and then the zoom lens just went into autological action. But in the end, it's the genius that's captured (or whatever word you want to use for a hyper-driven and prolific songwriter with a consistently high-quality output level). Let's also not forget the wild behavior that often comes with it all is exactly what everyone wants from rock-and-roll, or at least everyone in the times of this reality.

Back in the other corner, Courtney Taylor-Taylor of the Dandy Warhols has now flipped opinions on the doc from dig-able to denouncement after the avalanche of film and music critics alike almost universally dubbed the

Dandys the "sellouts" of the two groups, to which, *yeah*, uh, I mean, "whatever," but then Courtney—despite having narrated the whole thing in the first place—has now somehow become the victim of an apparent gigantic on-film charade. Hey, I feel all that, but I also do have to wonder if a thoughtful artists' profile of friends turned competitive musicians who'd at a certain point simply chosen to not help each in any way—in a divergent "see you in hell" separate musical journey paths way—would have had the same effect on the moviegoing masses that couldn't tear their eyes from what it had turned out to be. In the end, I don't want to ponder too much upon it all, as I—like the rest of them—am very much involved in this ballroom dance, wanting you to think I'm pretty.

Square Aliens

Then the current reality pageant continues to up the weird doses when I receive a phone call at my J-O-B, Amoeba Music, from someone representing Warner Brothers Television Studios down in Los Angeles. I'm told that the creators of a TV show called *The Gilmore Girls* are big fans of *Dig!* and are writing an episode with me in mind. Would I be interested in coming down to Hollywood and being a part of it? Play myself on network TV? "Sounds sorta kinda interesting," I say and give him my email, and the tambourine is rolling.

The show is a comedy-drama focusing on a single mother and teenage daughter, and word from some coworkers, it's apparently not just for the young-adult crowd, but also "hip" people my age and older, as it's supposed to be a "cool" pop-culture reference fest with Village Green–era Kinks being referenced in last week's episode. I watch the next new episode and find myself waiting for the *Twin Peaks* style wink, but I don't see it. Meanwhile, hidden from view inside of my face, my hurting tooth does see it and so we go ahead and get the dates from the casting director.

Then, over the next couple of weeks I find myself going back and forth on it, ultimately deciding that the one big thing I just can't abide by is the reality of what would surely be sharing the screen with eighties hair metal singer

Sebastian Bach from Skid Row, who is in the pretend band I'm supposed to join. I was a devout Jesus & Mary Chain kid growing up in the eighties and bands like Skid Row were the enemy. I can't get past it, so I decide to turn the offer down, making excuses that the dates they need me for don't work. These excuses are too flimsy to reproduce here but my thinking is that TV shows must run on tight schedules, and that will be that. But then the writer of the proposed episode comes back with a can of flimsy repellent, saying that they are willing to work around all of my excuses. They really wanted me for what was described as *"... basically a parody of what you really went through in BJM"* which he described as basically recreating our on-stage fight at the Viper Room.

I ask around the Amoeba staff of over a hundred pop culture enthusiasts and/or music snobs for their taste-maker opinions. All of my straight friends say I should do it because it would be weird, and my gay friends say "do it or I will kill you."

I'm abruptly woken up by the worst sound in the world, which is the shrill electric-chicken falsetto of a hotel room phone in the massive tourist ant farm that is whatever this Hollywood Universal Studios hotel is. It's 8:05 a.m., and apparently, I was supposed to have been supplied with an on-set call time of 7 a.m. so I could go through wardrobe and makeup and be on set five minutes ago. "Okay, well we're all here waiting on-set, so as soon as you can make it here ..." She is nice but "We're all here waiting" is what time it is, and time is money and there was nothing about an on-set time in the emails, which had me thinking I'd just stroll on in at a reasonable morning time, which now seems weird to me that I thought that.

Fifteen minutes later and I've slid down the Tambopole and am ready, but now there's no way for me to get the provided rental car out of the traffic-lightless hotel exit with six lanes of impatient rage racing back and forth. It's been so long now, I'm seriously starting to think about just gunning it, as this could be my last chance to die still cool. And if I die, I die, and this way maybe I'll go out like James Dean, minus doing it in an extremely cool car and some other stuff.

I eventually get to go, but I do it like Grace Kelly walking across a room wanting to be noticed, pinky pointed out the window, and then driving away from all the honking cars. My exit is already here so I just get off the freeway again pretty much immediately and into Toluca Lake to Warner Brothers Studios. To get in, I first must drive through what looks like a tollbooth with a security guard inside. The guard sees me coming and looks at me funny. Then I roll down the window and hand him my ID. He looks at it, looks at his clipboard, and then looks at me, then he does the whole routine again like he's either working out a kink in his neck or he's not totally sure he wants to let me in. Like it's the scene where I'm the undercover secret agent posing as an important scientist or something that secretly is here to stop the rocket launch inside.

I park in front of the designated soundstage that from outside looks like a massive tan airplane hangar. Slowly opening the side door, I poke my head inside, and it's an all-black interior of a small live rock venue full of people.

Dozens of extras are standing in front of a stage where musician actors are set up and ready to play. Around them all is a full television crew, and every single head in the room turns to look at who've they've all been standing around waiting for.

"Hi*iii*," I say, not yet committing to entering.

A friendly enough be-headsetted young lady comes over and then guides me to the side-stage steps as the room remains completely silent. I'm wondering if this is because I'm in trouble, when suddenly Sebastian Bach, in his cut-off tank top and blond metal hair breaks the silence. "*Dude! I loved you in that movie, man!*"

I'm grateful for this welcoming gesture and am put at ease by this person who once upon a time would have been my sworn enemy. Everyone below the stage comes back to life, and they make final preparations before we are to roll the first take.

After some quick on-stage introductions, I look down at my personal "X" in masking tape or "mark," adjust myself, and then a makeup girl powders on a once-over. My gaze wanders around the behind-the-scenes scene that's actually in front of the scene and everything seems whatever enough, except for the fact that my forward view here includes Sebastian Bach's giant, hairy back mole located below his shoulder. The hairs are two inches long and thick, sprouting from it like spider legs. He starts to riff on his unplugged Fender Strat, and as he does, the spider leg hairs begin to air guitar with him.

We do a take of me walking out on stage to join the TV band and the director immediately sees that I needeth not for direction, leaving me alone to discover my character. I decide to play it as if I were myself just being myself while acting as if I knew something stupid was going on.

Multiple takes are needed from various angles and I have to stand up there to lend a shoulder or an arm for the close-ups and other angles of each character's confusion, which is the theme of the scene. It's one that I am an expert on when of the on-stage persuasion, but this one is fake and not of the as-real-as-it-gets brand I've only ever known. This will be my inroad to utilizing the "Method" style of acting popularized by actors like Marlon Brando and Montgomery Clift. And this, I say to myself, will be my opus under-the-radar message to what will surely be for the entire worldwide intelligentsia watching at home. They will get my statement of purposeful lack of seriousness toward the whole affair and I will henceforth be a celebrated hero among them for my contribution in dismantling the mainstream media with aloof rebel facial-hair-covered antics.

We take a break and I meet Dan Paladino, husband to the show's creator, Amy Sherman-Palladino and the big *Dig!* fan I was in email correspondence with, who's written today's episode. "When you had to change dates, we had to reschedule Madeleine Albright for you!" He smiles, very humored by the fact, which also goes to show I'm never done sticking it to The Man, even when he's an old lady.

The crowd of crowd extras are all 86'd into the noontime after hours, but for me, it's back up on stage to do more angle shots. This goes on for hours, broken up by periodic breaks where I spend my down time in the star trailer I've been provided. There's not much to do in here unless you feel like some nuts or just want to sit and ponder being a star or something. I'd go over my lines, but they have kept them down to just three, which is the maximum I can have before they would be required to buy me a SAG card membership, which is a surprising cheap-skated-ness that will return again later.

Then it's time for the big fight scene, and here comes the stunt team with Sebastian Bach, who walks back up on stage smiling and looking mind blown in that "I can't believe how good this Van Halen guitar solo is" way that they do. He says to me, "*Dude!* After this, me and you are gonna smoke a *fat* J in my hotel room!" I appreciate this offer via a heads-up to start thinking of excuses, as this is the flimsy excuse-making period of my life and so the extra time to think of a good one always helps.

SB is going to do his own stunts for the fight scene and runs through, tackling his stuntman partner, who's dressed like the band's singer that is fake-possessed by the same real whatever it was Anton was possessed by at the Viper Room.

The scene is choreographed under the supervision of today's stunt team leader, an elder stunt dude who was around in the days of *The Six Million Dollar Man*. It's all very serious business for some reason and then I'm to go on stage to be a part of the "melee," while these two stunt-fight, which after a bunch of rehearsing weirdly exposes the original fight to have been a lot easier to get started.

"Action" is called and SB and the singer stunt double throw themselves into each other, but SB hits the ground weird and injures his leg. A man has gone down under the guard's watch and there is now a stoic air among the stunt team. They film a few more go's, now with a second stunt double donning a SB hair metal wig while I'm standing in the middle of the fighting, now wishing I'd asked Zoe from the *Kill Bill* movies to do this for me. Suddenly, there's another tense moment with the new Sebastian Bach, who thinks he may have just gotten a charley horse or something but then realizes it's wearing off already. The whole stunt team breathes a sigh of relief, and there's nothing left for them to do now. Soon after it's 5 p.m., and everyone is finally finished for the day.

I walk out of the soundstage and join the rest of the fake band, who've been off since the stage fight stunts started. Sebastian Bach already has purple wine lips going in the last twenty minutes since I saw him last and Spider Bach Mole is passed out drunk with legs hanging limp. I go to my trailer before sneaking away to the parking lot.

A month later, I go back down to Los Angeles to do the second episode. This one starts off way easier and much more like the movies always promised, driving around in a motorized cart up and down the avenues within the gigantic soundstages. Actor Todd Lowe, my on-screen besty-westy but real-life just nice-guy-I-don't-know-really, strums a Woody Guthrie song on guitar as we are driven to a "Main Street" set that's been in a thousand movies and television shows. Next to it is a fake neighborhood where the *Leave It to Beaver* house is, which is something for a second and then isn't again.

The director this time doesn't have it together as much as my last episode's director, who I forgot to mention has directed things like a Michael Jackson live television special, but she does allow me to improvise my scene, which gets all the extras and crew cracking up at my shimmy dancing and riffing some *Dig!*-esque goofing antics, which I give a different variation of for each take. Everyone is very pleased with my performance, except for the producers or whoever worries after the fact, and they are worried that once the episode airs, I'm going to come back and claim songwriter's publishing on my improv rants. So, to prevent this nefarious possible plan, which, to be honest with you, I could have never thought of, the whole bit is cut in half and I'm to redub my part with just standard uninteresting grunts of "Uh!" and "C'mon!"

So, to get this done and now that it's weeks later and I'm up in San Francisco, I have to go into a sound studio in the Barbary Coast area, which is a section of SF near North Beach where most of the television and radio broadcast stations are, to make my bit more boring, all because the show doesn't trust that I just want it to be good. They strip the audio, and my animated "feeling it" monologue turns into uninteresting, mismatched lip-syncing. I couldn't believe it. Then, the unbelieving continued further when, I guess because of the extra expense this all incurs, I'm suddenly taken off the invite list to the wedding episode with Sonic Youth and Sparks.

Despite my command performances, this whole experience tempts me to turn my back on television acting, yet what if by doing so, maybe I was playing right into the hands of Leonardo DiCaprio and his likely attempts at having my future Hollywood acting career blocked for good because of the *Star Wars* toys incident?

I walk into another Amoeba Music record store shift to find someone has printed out and taped a music website screenshot reviewing The Brian Jonestown Massacre's New York show the previous night. It was a picture of Anton during the show from the waist up, guitar strapped on and looking right at the camera. Underneath was a quote from a girl who had cried out, "I miss Joel!", something I would later find out had become a repeated nightly occurrence. Underneath her angelic majesty's request was his reply, "Well, why don't you go to fuckin' Amoeba Records and visit him? And while you're there, buy a record so he doesn't get fired!"

Then magically, about a week later …

JOEL GION

will return in

IT TAKES TWO JINGLES TO JANGLE

PRAISE FOR IN THE JINGLE JANGLE JUNGLE:

RESIDENT'S BOOK OF THE YEAR 2024

A ROUGH TRADE BOOK OF THE YEAR 2024

"Rock 'n' roll book of the decade!"

    CHRIS ROBINSON

"[Joel's] got me glued to these pages … I think my brother

knows how to feel."

    KURT VILE